YOUR PERSONAL STRESS PROFILE

AND ACTIVITY WORKBOOK

YOUR PERSONAL STRESS PROFILE AND ACTIVITY WORKBOOK

Fourth Edition

Jerrold S. Greenberg
University of Maryland

Boston   Burr Ridge, IL   Dubuque, IA   Madison, WI   New York   San Francisco   St. Louis
Bangkok   Bogotá   Caracas   Kuala Lumpur   Lisbon   London   Madrid   Mexico City
Milan   Montreal   New Delhi   Santiago   Seoul   Singapore   Sydney   Taipei   Toronto

Higher Education

3 4 5 6 7 8 9 0 QPD/QPD 0 9 8 7

ISBN-13: 978-0-07-310675-5
ISBN-10: 0-07-310675-5

Editor in Chief: *Emily Barrosse*
Publisher: *Bill Glass*
Sponsoring Editor: *Nicholas Barrett*
Director of Development: *Kate Engelberg*
Senior Developmental Editor: *Michelle A. Turenne*
Executive Marketing Manager: *Pamela S. Cooper*
Editorial and Marketing Coordinator: *Nancy Null*
Managing Editor: *Jean Dal Porto*
Project Manager: *Emily Hatteberg*
Art Director: *Jeanne Schreiber*
Associate Designer: *Srdjan Savanovic*
Cover Designer: *JoAnne Schopler*
Cover Credit: *© Corbis*
Technology Development Editor: *Julia Ersery*
Media Producer: *Lance Gerhart*
Media Project Manager: *Ron Nelms*
Production Supervisor: *Janean A. Utley*
Composition: *11/13 Times Roman by Cenveo*
Printing: *45 # Scholarly Matte Recycled, Quebecor World Dubuque Inc.*

The Internet addresses listed in the text were accurate at the time of publication. The inclusion of a website does not indicate an endorsement by the authors of McGraw-Hill, and McGraw-Hill does not guarantee the accuracy of the information presented at these sites.

www.mhhe.com

Contents

Preface

When Rabbi Hirshel Jaffe crossed the finish line of the New York City Marathon in 1978, little did he know that he would soon face the toughest race of his life, the race against cancer. His subsequent victory over leukemia gave him a special mission—to help others overcome adversity as he had.

Rabbi Jaffe began counseling cancer patients. He became co-editor of a magazine, *Gates of Healing,* which is distributed to hospital patients everywhere, and wrote a highly acclaimed book entitled *Why Me, Why Anyone?* As if that wasn't enough, Rabbi Jaffe developed a videotape for cancer patients entitled *Hanging on to Hope.* It is not surprising that in 1988 he received the American Cancer Society's "Award of Courage" from President Ronald Reagan.

But when Jaffe, who serves as rabbi of Temple Beth Jacob in Newburgh, New York, talks about overcoming adversity, he's not just referring to physical illness. In 1980 he visited our hostages in Iran to give them comfort and support. And in October 1992 he led a "Unity March" in Newburgh protesting the appearance of the Ku Klux Klan in his town. Over 3,000 people, from all over New York State, participated in that march.

Among those who know him best, Hirshel Jaffe in known as "the Running Rabbi" not just for his marathons, but for his tireless efforts on behalf of others.

Rabbi Hirshel Jaffe experienced a stressful situation, but rather than assume the role of victim, he decided he would manage his stress by using his diagnosis to make his life even more meaningful than it had been to that point. There are many different ways of managing stress. Rabbi Jaffe found a way that worked for him. Have you found a way that works for you? This book will help you in that quest.

Your Personal Stress Profile and Activity Workbook is designed to meet two basic purposes. First, it will allow you to evaluate yourself relative to stress. That is, you will develop a personal stress profile based on your responses to 25 stress-related scales. Most of these scales were either developed for and/or appear in *An Evaluation Handbook for Health Education Programs in Stress Management* published by the Centers for Disease Control of the U.S. government.* This stress profile will include the following components:

1. Your typical response to stress.
2. How much you know about stress.
3. How often you use effective stress management strategies.
4. How satisfied you are with your life.
5. Your skills in communicating about stress.
6. The nature of and degree to which you experience stressful feelings.
7. Your effectiveness in employing relaxation techniques to manage stress.
8. Your ability to employ systematic decision-making skills to manage stress.
9. Your intention to use stress management techniques.

*Centers for Disease Control. *An Evaluation Handbook for Health Education Programs in Stress Management.* Washington, DC: Department of Health and Human Services, 1983.

The second purpose of *Your Personal Stress Profile and Activity Workbook* is to provide activities you can use to improve stress-related components on which you scored low. Interpret your scores and decide where you need improvement. Activities appearing in each section of the workbook are a good start for working on these components. Your instructor may be able to recommend even more activities that you can use to improve your stress profile so you can enjoy a less stressful life.

Changes over Four Editions

Your Personal Stress Profile and Activity Workbook has changed significantly from the first edition to its current fourth edition. Originally, the organization was not specifically related to the text that might accompany *Your Personal Stress Profile and Activity Workbook.* Although this workbook can stand on its own, it is clearly coordinated with the text *Comprehensive Stress Management,* now in its ninth edition. That allows you to explore your relationship to stress and stress management even more completely than before through placement of a workbook icon, which shows relevant page numbers from the workbook. Icons in the text refer you to places in the workbook that relate to the content the text presents.

In addition, several scales and numerous activities have been added over the years. In fact, seven scales appear in the current edition of *Your Personal Stress Profile and Activity Workbook* that were not included in the first edition. Along with these scales, you will find activities specifically designed to engage you in an interesting and educational manner, helping you improve the stress-related variables measured by the scales. In this way, your stress profile will be more complete.

Still, the intent of *Your Personal Stress Profile and Activity Workbook* remains the same over its four editions: namely, to relate stress to you personally and to help you acquire the skills to better manage the stress of your life. Let's proceed to actually do that.

Acknowledgments

We would be remiss without acknowledging the assistance of the publisher's reviewers for their helpful input: Guy E. Cunningham, PhD, Grand View College and Rick B. Lambson EdD, Southern Utah University. We truly appreciate their valuable comments and suggestions to this fourth edition.

Introduction: Can We Talk?

Robert Redford, Richard Gere, and Danny DeVito all die on the same day. A cursory review of their lives brings them to the doors of Dante's inferno. As their guide brings them to their eternal dwellings, he starts with Robert Redford. "Robert, because you made millions of dollars and hid in the mountains of Utah rather than share your wealth with homeless people, you will forever abide in this room." He escorts Redford to a room in which a violin player is "screeching" the strings, making an ear-piercing, unbearable sound. Next, Richard Gere is brought to a room with someone running chalk on a chalkboard, thereby making a "teeth-shattering, bone-chilling" sound. "Richard, because you ran around with hundreds of women, you are forever assigned to live in this room." Lastly, Danny DeVito is escorted to a room, where he is surprised to see Kim Basinger lying nude on a bed. As they enter the room, the guide sternly says, "Kim, because of your behavior, you are forever assigned to abide with Danny DeVito." Which only proves that life, and maybe even what happens afterward, is unpredictable.

It is this unpredictability that can be stressful, and there is an abundance of research to support this conclusion. This workbook is designed to walk you through the various aspects of stress and stress management so, by the time you are through, you will be better able to handle the unpredictable events in your life. In fact, you may come to relish them.

But, first, let's understand each other. Life is too short for me to have written this workbook for you to "blow it off." And it is too short for you to waste your time completing it just to get it done. So let's work together to do something meaningful with the time you spend on this workbook. Let's travel together down the road to a more satisfied you. Let me be your guide. There may not be a Kim Basinger or a Richard Gere at the end of the road, but there will be greater insight about how you interact with the stress in your life and how you can manage it better.

I really do want to help you manage stress better! Do you really want to let me help? If so, let's begin by determining how you presently react to stressful situations and discuss how your reactions might be even more effective.

Section **1**   **Your Typical Response to Stress**

We all find ourselves in stressful situations from time to time. If we didn't, life would be a bore. It would be too predictable, too routine, and because of that, it would be stressful. It is not that we have stress that is the problem; it is that we do not respond to or manage it well. Some people become aggressive when that is an inappropriate reaction. These are the people who get into fights, either verbal or physical. Others make poor decisions in an attempt to manage the stress. They may drink alcohol or use other drugs to alleviate the stress. Yet, when the drug wears off, the stressful situation or feelings remain. Still others ignore the need to act altogether. This "head in the sand" approach to coping is usually ineffective since, as when drugs are used, the situation remains unchanged, waiting for the head to resurface.

     Do any of these descriptions apply to you? To help you answer that question, and to assess how you typically react to stress, we present the *Appropriate Response to Stress* scale.

Scale 1.1: How Effective Would You Be in Responding to Stressful Situations?

Using the scale below, you can determine whether your responses to specific stressful situations would be appropriate. If not, the scale helps you determine whether your responses would be unhealthy, a direct violation of appropriate response, a denial, or outright ineffective.

> This test presents descriptions of people in stressful situations. These people want to reduce their stress. Read each item. Circle the letter of the appropriate action for the person to take to reduce the stress. If there is no appropriate choice presented, circle choice D, "None of the above."

1.   Valerie has just been promoted to a new job in a different city. An appropriate way for Valerie to reduce her stress would be to:
    A.   change her hairstyle and way of dressing to reflect her new image.
    B.   take on as much work as she can to keep herself busy.
    C.   establish a suitable schedule soon after she arrives.
    D.   None of the above.

2.   John is in a noisy office and is trying to concentrate on his work. An appropriate way for John to reduce his stress would be to:
    A.   skip lunch and work during the lunch hour when the office is quieter.
    B.   rearrange the books and papers on his desk.
    C.   wear more comfortable clothes to work.
    D.   None of the above.

3. Bruce is worried that he will fail his history test, even though he has studied hard for it. An appropriate way for Bruce to reduce his stress would be to:
   A. stay up late the night before the test in order to study more.
   B. think about how angry his parents will be if he fails the test.
   C. go out and take a bicycle ride.
   D. None of the above.

4. Arthur is very busy typing when a co-worker asks Arthur to help her with her typing. Arthur is a bit annoyed by her request. An appropriate way for Arthur to reduce his stress would be to:
   A. help her with her typing but explain that he won't do it again.
   B. explain that he can't do her typing and concentrate on finishing his own work.
   C. pretend that his co-worker's request doesn't bother him and continue working.
   D. None of the above.

5. Paul has been told that there is no chance that he can pitch for his baseball team because the owner's son will be taking his place. An appropriate way for Paul to reduce his stress would be to:
   A. look into pitching for another team.
   B. get to know the other members of the team better.
   C. tell the owner that he insists on being able to pitch for the team, no matter what.
   D. None of the above.

6. Nancy drives home on a busy, crowded freeway. An appropriate way for Nancy to reduce her stress would be to:
   A. drive with the car windows open slightly.
   B. make sure that she takes the same route home whenever possible.
   C. drink a cup of coffee as she drives.
   D. None of the above.

7. Gary is concerned that the quality of his work is not good enough, even though all of the people he works with tell him he's doing a good job. An appropriate way for Gary to reduce his stress would be to:
   A. spend more time trying to improve the quality of his work.
   B. plan to have a few beers with his co-workers every day after work.
   C. spend more time focusing on the positive qualities of his work.
   D. None of the above.

8. Leslie has just recently married and moved to a new city. An appropriate way for Leslie to reduce her stress would be to:
   A. try to change some of her old habits.
   B. set aside some time each day to relax.
   C. take a vacation with her husband.
   D. None of the above.

9. Sharon works on an assembly line where she watches metal fittings go by all day long. An appropriate way for Sharon to reduce her stress would be to:
   A. bring in a soft cushion for her chair.
   B. ask her boss if she can listen to a radio as she works.
   C. see if she can work through lunch so that she can finish her work as quickly as possible.
   D. None of the above.

10. Karen had been planning on taking a week off from work. Now her boss tells Karen that it is impossible for her to have the vacation time she had planned. An appropriate way for Karen to reduce her stress would be to:
    A. threaten to switch jobs unless she can take her vacation as planned.
    B. act as if she didn't want the time off that much anyway.
    C. tell her boss that she's disappointed and ask if she can take the time off next month.
    D. None of the above.

11. Phyllis has four final exams and only two days left to study for them. An appropriate way for Phyllis to reduce her stress would be to:
    A. take her mind off her own tests by helping a friend study.
    B. pick the hardest course and study for that exam only.
    C. set up a schedule so that she has some time to study for each test.
    D. None of the above.

12. Gwen wants to be president of a local club but has been told that she doesn't have the organizational ability. An appropriate way for Gwen to reduce her stress would be to:
    A. stop attending club meetings.
    B. take a business class to improve her skills.
    C. tell the club members that she doesn't really want to be president.
    D. None of the above.

13. Gregg lives across from an all-night gas station and is disturbed by the noise from the cars. An appropriate way for Gregg to reduce his stress would be to:
    A. play loud music to block out the noise.
    B. take a sleeping pill to help get to sleep.
    C. give all of his business to another gas station.
    D. None of the above.

14. Stanley is surrounded by people at a very crowded party. An appropriate way for Stanley to reduce his stress would be to:
    A. stay in the middle of the crowd.
    B. have several extra glasses of wine in order to relax.
    C. loosen his tie so that he will feel more comfortable.
    D. None of the above.

15. Joyce must speak to a large group of people and keeps thinking about the time she was giving a speech in front of her class and forgot what she was to say. An appropriate way for Joyce to reduce her stress would be to:
   A. set aside some time before the speech to relax.
   B. remember as many details as she can about her previous experience giving a speech.
   C. keep her hands busy while she gives the speech.
   D. None of the above.

SCORING*

Assign yourself one point for each of the following responses:

1.	C		9.	B
2.	D		10.	C
3.	C		11.	C
4.	B		12.	B
5.	A		13.	D
6.	D		14.	D
7.	C		15.	A
8.	B			

These are the appropriate responses to each situation described. If you made other choices, you did not react the most effective way. You might have reacted in an unhealthy way, as when you skip lunch to reduce stress resulting from a noisy work environment as in the situation described in item 2. Or you may have chosen an ineffective response, as when you take on as much work as you can to keep busy when overwhelmed with stress from a new job in a new city as in situation 1. Another response might have been a direct violation of what would be an appropriate response, such as when you decide to think about how angry your parents would be to your failing a test as in situation 3. Or you may have used outright denial as when you are annoyed by a co-worker's request but pretend it doesn't bother you as in situation 4.

INTERPRETATION OF SCORES

This scale measures how effective you would be in responding to stressful situations. Using the key below, you can evaluate your incorrect answers as being either:

1. *Unhealthy*—a response that is unhealthy.
2. *Direct Violation*—a response that is in direct violation of the appropriate responses to stress.
3. *Denial*—a response that denies the stress or the problem producing the stress.
4. *Ineffective*—a response that is related to the situation but is ineffective in reducing stress. It is neither unhealthy, nor in direct violation, nor denial.
5. *None of the Above*—a response that indicates there is no correct answer when there is a correct answer.

* *Source:* Centers for Disease Control. *An Evaluation Handbook for Health Education Programs in Stress Management.* Washington, DC: Department of Health and Human Services, 1983, pp. 105–112.

INCORRECT ANSWER CHOICE ANALYSIS

	Unhealthy	Direct Violation	Denial	Ineffective	None of the Above
1.	—	A	—	B	D
2.	A	—	—	B,C	—
3.	A	B	—	—	D
4.	—	A	C	—	D
5.	—	C	—	B	D
6.	C	—	—	A,B	—
7.	B	—	—	A	D
8.	—	A,C	—	—	D
9.	C	—	—	A	D
10.	—	A	B	—	D
11.	—	A	—	B	D
12.	—	—	C	A	D
13.	B	A	—	C	—
14.	B	A	—	C	—
15.	—	B	—	C	D

ACTIVITY: SELECTIVE AWARENESS

One very appropriate response to stress that has been demonstrated to be effective is called *selective awareness*. Selective awareness is learning to perceive life changes and other stressors as less distressing by attending to their *positive* aspects and de-emphasizing their *negative* ones. We all are free to choose what to think, although most of us don't exercise this control of our thoughts but allow them to ride the high seas rudderless. To complicate matters, we have been taught to be critical rather than supportive, focusing on the bad rather than the good. To help you learn to focus on the positive aspects of situations and people, rephrase the following situations so the focus is upon their positive components:

1.   Waiting in a long line to attend a movie

   _____

   _____

2.   Being stuck in bumper-to-bumper traffic

   _____

   _____

3.   Having to make a presentation before a group of people

   _____

   _____

4. Being rejected from something because you're too old

_____

_____

5. Having a relationship break up

_____

_____

Right now there are situations in your life that are causing you a great deal of stress. You may not like where you live, or with whom you're living, or the work you're doing. You may not feel you have enough time to yourself or for leisure activities. You may not like the way you look. You may be in poor health. You may be alone. Some of these stressors you may be able to change; some you will not be able to change. You now know, however, that you can become selectively aware of their positive components while de-emphasizing (though not denying) their disturbing features. Below, list these stressors, and list the positive aspects of each upon which you will choose to focus:

SELECTIVE AWARENESS: Stressors and Their Positive Aspects

1. Stressor: _____
   Positive Aspect: _____
2. Stressor: _____
   Positive Aspect: _____
3. Stressor: _____
   Positive Aspect: _____

Why not go even further? Each time you do something that works out well, keep the memory of that with you. Tell others how proud of yourself you are. Pat yourself on the back. Take time just before bed (or some other convenient time of day) to recall all the good things about that day. Don't be like some of your friends who can't sleep because they still feel embarrassed about something they did that day or worried about something over which they have no control. In the words of a best seller of several years ago, "Be your own best friend." Revel in your good points and the glory of your day.

Section **II**   **What Is Stress? Your Stress Knowledge**

This section measures how much you know about stress and how much you know about how to manage stress effectively. If you don't know enough about stress and its causes, nor about the best ways to manage the stress you experience, you are more likely to have that stress develop into negative consequences. Such consequences can include threats to your health (for example, hypertension, heart disease, or headaches), difficulty concentrating on your job or schoolwork, or impatience and tension that interfere with your interpersonal relationships.

Scale 2.1: How Much Do You Know About Stress and Its Effects?

How much do you know about stress? Its causes? Its effects? This scale will help you determine your level of stress knowledge.

This test consists of 20 statements about stress. Some of the statements are true and some are false. If you think a statement is true, put a check in the column labeled True. If you think a statement is false, put a check in the column labeled False.

TRUE   FALSE
_____   _____   1. People react to psychosocial stressors.
_____   _____   2. Constant arousal due to stress can cause a person's blood pressure to remain at a low level.
_____   _____   3. Stress due to overload can result from demands that occur at home.
_____   _____   4. An individual who is adjusting to many life changes in a short period of time is less likely than usual to become ill.
_____   _____   5. Thinking about an unpleasant event is never as stressful as actually experiencing the event.
_____   _____   6. Thinking of oneself as useless and powerless can increase one's stress level.
_____   _____   7. The most stressful situations are usually those over which people feel they have a great deal of control.
_____   _____   8. Stress may decrease the body's ability to defend itself against disease.
_____   _____   9. Severe stress may cause people to have accidents.
_____   _____   10. One of the most common traits of the Type A personality is doing only one thing at a time.
_____   _____   11. Excessive stress probably decreases the rate at which one's body uses up vitamin C.

		12.	A person under stress may feel confused.
___	___	13.	Overload occurs when people are able to meet the demands that are placed on them.
___	___	14.	A person under stress is often able to perform tasks better than usual.
___	___	15.	Some degree of stress is necessary for life.
___	___	16.	Stress can lead to the failure of organ systems in the body.
___	___	17.	Too much stimulation is always more stressful than too little.
___	___	18.	High blood pressure can injure the heart even though there are no obvious symptoms.
___	___	19.	The stress produced by a situation depends more on the situation itself than on the person's perception of the situation.
___	___	20.	The Type A personality is associated with heart disease.

SCORING*

Assign yourself one point for each of the following responses:

Item	Answer	Item	Answer
1	T	11	F
2	F	12	T
3	T	13	F
4	F	14	F
5	F	15	T
6	T	16	T
7	F	17	F
8	T	18	T
9	T	19	F
10	F	20	T

INTERPRETATION OF SCORES

So, how did you do? If you scored higher than 11, you did pretty well. If you scored lower than 11, you need to learn more about stress. Perhaps you didn't realize that stress can make your blood pressure rise, or that the stress resulting from having to adjust to many life changes subjects you to illnesses, or that thinking about an unpleasant event can be worse than actually experiencing it. You may not have known that low self-esteem can be stressful, or that not having control of a situation is usually more stressful than when you can exercise some degree of control, or that stress can lower the effectiveness of your immunological system resulting in your becoming ill. Then again, you

*Source: Centers for Disease Control. *An Evaluation Handbook for Health Education Programs in Stress Management.* Washington, DC: Department of Health and Human Services, 1983, pp. 89–92.

may never have heard that stress can lead to accidents or confusion, or that some degree of stress is necessary in everyone's life. Were you surprised to learn that too little stimulation may be even more stressful than too much, or that a situation often becomes more stressful because of how you perceive it than because of the situation itself, or that a certain personality may be associated with heart disease?

There are many books written about stress that can provide you with the information you need. I have even authored one of these: *Comprehensive Stress Management.* There are classes in community centers, and college courses, and workshops at places of work that teach about stress and stress management. You may want to consider one or more of these experiences to expand your knowledge about a very important aspect of your life.

ACTIVITY: READING ABOUT STRESS

One way to learn more about stress and stress management is to read a book about these topics. Below is a short list of books on these subjects:

Cottrell, Randall R. *Stress Management.* Guilford, CT: Dushkin Publishing Group, 1992.
Girdano, Daniel A., Everly, George S., and Dusek, Dorothy E. *Controlling Stress and Tension.* 6th ed. Boston: Allyn and Bacon, 2001.
Greenberg, Jerrold S. *Comprehensive Stress Management.* 9th ed. New York: Mcgraw-Hill, 2006.
Greenberg, Jerrold S. *Coping with Stress: A Practical Guide.* Dubuque, IA: Wm. C. Brown, 1990.
Monat, Alan, and Lazarus, Richard S. *Stress and Coping: An Anthology.* 3rd ed. New York: Columbia University Press, 1991.
Rice, Phillip L. *Stress and Health.* 3rd ed. Pacific Grove, CA: Brooks/Cole, 1999.
Schafer, Walt. *Stress Management for Wellness.* Orlando, FL: Harcourt Brace Jovanovich, 1992.

Scale 2.2: How Much Do You Know About How to Manage Stress Effectively?

Okay, so you now know something about stress and its effects. Knowledge like this is only valuable if it provides guidance to improve your life. Knowing that sticky foods that cling to your teeth can cause tooth decay is useless unless you know how to get the sticky stuff off by brushing and flossing properly. The same is true with stress. Knowing what causes it and how it can affect you is only part of the story. Do you know what to do to manage the stress you experience so it doesn't make you ill or harm you in other ways? To find out, complete the *Coping with Stress* scale on the following page.

This test consists of 20 statements about stress. Some of the statements are true and some are false. If you think a statement is true, put a check in the column labeled True. If you think a statement is false, put a check in the column labeled False.

TRUE	FALSE		
____	____	1.	Imagining heaviness and warmth in one's body parts is an autogenic training technique.
____	____	2.	An individual should consume more caffeine during stressful times.
____	____	3.	Competitive physical activity is an effective stress management technique.
____	____	4.	Involvement in the pleasure of physical activity leads to feelings of well-being.
____	____	5.	Breaking down complicated tasks into smaller parts can reduce stress.
____	____	6.	Stress can be reduced by avoiding routines whenever possible.
____	____	7.	When undergoing important life changes, stress can be reduced by increasing the number of other changes that are made.
____	____	8.	Heartbeat can be monitored by biofeedback.
____	____	9.	Individuals should not try to change their relation to stressors.
____	____	10.	Sitting comfortably helps to quiet one's internal environment.
____	____	11.	Autogenic training is an effective technique for relieving vascular problems associated with stress.
____	____	12.	Anticipating periods of boredom and planning activities for those periods can reduce stress.
____	____	13.	When using physical exercise as a stress management technique, one should try to exert oneself as much as possible.
____	____	14.	In autogenic training, an individual attempts to eliminate the physical sensations that are associated with relaxation.
____	____	15.	Becoming less competitive with oneself and others is an effective way to reduce Type A behavior.
____	____	16.	Delegating authority and responsibility to others will have no effect on one's stress.
____	____	17.	To be effective, relaxation must be used at the same time and place each time it is done.
____	____	18.	Being in a place away from other people helps to quiet one's external environment.
____	____	19.	Focusing on one's positive characteristics improves a person's self-concept.
____	____	20.	Increased muscle activity is a characteristic of relaxation.

SCORING*

Assign yourself one point for each of the following responses:

Item	Answer	Item	Answer
1	T	11	T
2	F	12	T
3	F	13	F
4	T	14	F
5	T	15	T
6	F	16	F
7	F	17	F
8	T	18	T
9	F	19	T
10	T	20	F

INTERPRETATION OF SCORES

This scale measures how much you know about how to effectively manage stress. The higher the score, the more you know about effectively managing stress. If you scored lower than 11, you need to learn more about this topic. Perhaps you never heard of autogenic training, or that caffeine can make stress worse, or that physical activity can help you manage stress, but competitive physical activity can actually increase the stress you experience. Maybe you never realized that stress can be reduced by making your life more routine, or that sitting comfortably can help quiet your internal environment, or that delegating authority and responsibility can help alleviate stress. Maybe you never heard of biofeedback, or that focusing on your positive aspects can make you feel less stressful, or that stress can make your muscles tense. Yet, these are all true and, knowing that, you can now use this knowledge to manage stress better.

ACTIVITY: USING TAPES/CONSULTING BOOKS

The best ways to increase your knowledge of stress-related information are immersing yourself in reading about stress, attending stress management workshops, or enrolling in stress management courses at a local college or university. As an alternative, you might want to consider the purchase of audiotapes or videotapes that concern themselves with some aspect of stress or stress management. A list of such tapes appears below, as does a listing of selected books that pertain to stress and/or stress management. As you sort through these materials, consider identifying at least one method you will use to

---

* *Source:* Centers for Disease Control. *An Evaluation Handbook for Health Education Programs in Stress Management.* Washington, DC: Department of Health and Human Services, 1983, pp. 97–100.

1. Change your *life* to eliminate a stressor (such as driving on a less crowded road).
2. Change your *perception* of a stressor so you consider it less distressing (such as focusing on the good in a situation).
3. Manage your *emotions* to a stressor (such as meditate).
4. *Use* the built-up by-products of stress (such as exercise).

STRESS MANAGEMENT AUDIOTAPES, VIDEOTAPES, AND BOOKS

AUDIOTAPES

"Beating the Blues." American Health Products, Dept. A894, Box 11271, Des Moines, Iowa 50340

"Cognitive Control Cassette Tapes." New Harbinger Publications, 5674 Shattuck Avenue, Oakland, California 94690

"Conquer the Fear of Public Speaking." Psychology Today Tapes, Dept. 964, Box 059073, Brooklyn, New York 11205-9061

"Deep Relaxation." Psychology Today Tapes, Dept. 964, Box 059073, Brooklyn, New York 11205-9061

"Effective Self-Assertion." Psychology Today Tapes, Dept. 964, Box 059073, Brooklyn, New York 11205-9061

"Exercises for Mind Expansion." Psychology Today Tapes, Dept. 964, Box 059073, Brooklyn, New York 11205-9061

"Getting Rid of Your Fears." Psychology Today Tapes, Dept. 964, Box 059073, Brooklyn, New York 11205-9061

"A Guide to Happiness." Psychology Today Tapes, Dept. 964, Box 059073, Brooklyn, New York 11205-9061

"How to Build Self-Esteem." Psychology Today Tapes, Dept. 964, Box 059073, Brooklyn, New York 11205-9061

"How to Stop Worrying and Start Living." Psychology Today Tapes, Dept. 964, Box 059073, Brooklyn, New York 11205-9061

"Hypnosis Tapes." New Harbinger Publications, 5674 Shattuck Avenue, Oakland, California 94609

"Learn to Relax: A 14-Day Program." Coulee Press, P.O. Box 1744, LaCrosse, Wisconsin 54602-1744

"Letting Go of Stress." Source Cassettes, 945 Evelyn Street, Menlo Park, California 94025

"Maintaining Self-Esteem." Psychology Today Tapes, Dept. 964, Box 059073, Brooklyn, New York 11205-9061

"Meditation: A Sensible Guide to a Timeless Discipline." Research Press, Box 3177, Dept. K, Champaign, Illinois 61821-9988

"Meditation—An Instructional Cassette." Psychology Today Tapes, Dept. 964, Box 059073, Brooklyn, New York 11205-9061

"Mental Imagery: Techniques and Exercises." Psychology Today Tapes, Dept. 964, Box 059073, Brooklyn, New York 11205-9061

"Mental Imagery: Your Hidden Potential." Psychology Today Tapes, Dept. 964, Box 059073, Brooklyn, New York 11205-9061

"Natural Ocean Soundtrack." Route 8, Box 78, High Point, North Carolina 27260

"Nobody Is Perfect." Psychology Today Tapes, Dept. 964, Box 059073, Brooklyn, New York 11205-9061

"Overcoming Shyness." Psychology Today Tapes, Dept. 964, Box 059073, Brooklyn, New York 11205-9061

"Peak Performance." Psychology Today Tapes, Dept. 964, Box 059073, Brooklyn, New York 11205-9061

"The Power of Self-Esteem." Audio-Forum, Dept. 542, Guilford, Connecticut 06437

"Progressive Relaxation." Psychology Today Tapes, Dept. 964, Box 059073, Brooklyn, New York 11205-9061

"Progressive Relaxation Training." Psychology Today Tapes, Dept. 964, Box 059073, Brooklyn, New York 11205-9061

"Relaxation & Stress Reduction Cassette Tapes." New Harbinger Publications, 5674 Shattuck Avenue, Oakland, California 94609

"Relaxation Dynamics." Research Press, Box 3177, Dept. K, Champaign, Illinois 61821-9988

"The Relaxed Body Cassette I for Muscle Relaxation." American Health Products, Dept. A90214, Box 11271, Des Moines, Iowa 50340

"The Relaxed Body Cassette II for Mental Relaxation." American Health Products, Dept. A90214, Box 11271, Des Moines, Iowa 50340

"Release Shoulder Tension." Kareena, do Yoga to Conga Drums, 1055 Pratt #3, Chicago, Illinois 60626

"The Self-Esteem Tapes." The Self-Esteem Tapes, Dept. A, 600 W. Grand, Suite 106, Hot Springs, Arkansas 71901

"Self-Relaxation Training." Research Press, Box 3177, Dept. K, Champaign, Illinois 61821-9988

"A Six-Second Technique to Control Stress." Psychology Today Tapes, Dept. 964, Box 059073, Brooklyn, New York 11205-9061

"Ten-Minute Stress Manager." Source Cassettes, 945 Evelyn Street, Menlo Park, California 94025

"Transforming Stress into Power." HEALTH EDCO, P.O. Box 21207, Waco, Texas 76702-1207

"Two Techniques for Treating Stress Disorders." Psychology Today Tapes, Dept. 964, Box 059073, Brooklyn, New York 11205-9061

"Understanding and Coping with Anxiety." Psychology Today Tapes, Dept. 964, Box 059073, Brooklyn, New York 11205-9061

"Visualization: Accessing the Higher Self." Psychology Today Tapes, Dept. 964, Box 059073, Brooklyn, New York 11205-9061

VIDEOTAPES

"Attacking Anxiety." Veritas Programming, Ltd., Order Center, 175 Fifth Avenue, Suite 2548, New York, New York 10010

"Coping: Ways to Handle Stress I." Queue, Inc., 562 Boston Avenue, Room 5, Bridgeport, Connecticut 06610

"Coping: Ways to Handle Stress II." Queue, Inc., 562 Boston Avenue, Room 5, Bridgeport, Connecticut 06610

"Fitness: Getting It All Back." American Health Products, Dept. A90214, Box 11271, Des Moines, Iowa 50340

"Male Stress Syndrome." Films for the Humanities and Sciences, Inc., Box 2053, Princeton, New Jersey 08543

"Managing Stress." Films for the Humanities and Sciences, Inc., Box 2053, Princeton, New Jersey 08543

"Managing Stress, Anxiety and Frustration." Human Relations Media, Room HC 123, 175 Tompkins Avenue, Pleasantville, New York 10570-9973

"Massage Your Mate." Ozman, Inc., 496-A Hudson Street, #K-17, New York 10004

"Our Nation under Stress." Films for the Humanities and Sciences, Inc., Box 2053, Princeton, New Jersey 08543

"Phobias." Films for the Humanities and Sciences, Inc., Box 2053, Princeton, New Jersey 08543

"Progressive Relaxation Training." Research Press, Box 3177, Dept. R, Champaign, Illinois 61821

"The Relaxed Body Video." American Health Products, Dept. A90214, Box 11271, Des Moines, Iowa 50340

"Stress: A Personal Challenge." Coronet/MTI Film & Video, 108 Wilmot Road, Deerfield, Illinois 60015

"Stress and Immune Function." Films for the Humanities and Sciences, Inc., Box 2053, Princeton, New Jersey 08543

"Stress in the Later Years." Kent State University, Audio Visual Services, Kent, Ohio 44242

"Stress: Is Your Lifestyle Killing You." Kent State University, Audio Visual Services, Kent, Ohio 44242

"Stress Management." Great Performance, Inc., 700 N. Green, Chicago, Illinois 60622

"The Stress Test." Kent State University, Audio Visual Services, Kent, Ohio 44242

"Stress: You Can Live with It." Coronet/MTI Film & Video, 108 Wilmot Road, Deerfield, Illinois 60015

"Stressbreak." Source Cassettes, 945 Evelyn Street, Menlo Park, California 94025

"Teens Dealing with Stress." Queue, Inc., 562 Boston Avenue, Room S, Bridgeport, Connecticut 06610

"The Time Bomb Within." Coronet/MTI Film & Video, 108 Wilmot Road, Deerfield, Illinois 60015

"Time Management." Wisconsin Clearinghouse, University of Wisconsin–Madison, Dept. CF, P.O. Box 1468, Madison, Wisconsin 53701

"Transforming Stress into Power." HEALTH EDCO, P.O. Box 21207, Waco, Texas 76702-1207

"What the World Dishes Out." Coronet/MTI Film & Video, 108 Wilmot Road, Deerfield, Illinois 60015

"What You Bring on Yourself." Coronet/MTI Film & Video, 108 Wilmot Road, Deerfield, Illinois 60015

"Women and Stress." Films for the Humanities and Sciences, Inc., Box 2053, Princeton, New Jersey 08543

"Yoga: Volume I—Beginners." Rudra Press, P.O. Box 1973-A, Cambridge, Massachusetts 02238

"Yoga: Volume II—Intermediates." Rudra Press, P.O. Box 1973-A, Cambridge, Massachusetts 02238

BOOKS

Allen, Roger J. *Human Stress: Its Nature and Control.* Minneapolis, MN: Burgess, 1983.

Benson, Herbert. *The Relaxation Response.* New York: Avon Books, 1985.

Charlesworth, Edward A., and Nathan, Ronald G. *Stress Management: A Comprehensive Guide to Wellness.* Houston, TX: Biobehavioral Publishers, 1982.

Friedman, Meyer, and Rosenman, Ray H. *Type A Behavior and Your Heart.* Greenwich, CT: Fawcett, 1974.

Woolfolk, R., and Lehrer, P. (eds.). *Principles and Practices of Stress Management.* New York: Guilford Press, 1984.

Section III Setting Up Stress Roadblocks: Using Stress Management Techniques

Carlos was invited to dinner by Maria, the most gorgeous woman he had ever met. When he arrived at her apartment, Maria told him she was still getting dressed so he should make himself comfortable for a while. Wanting to impress her with his sensitivity and good nature, Carlos played with her dog as he waited. He quickly realized this was no ordinary dog. Fido could field balls thrown to him better than any baseball player he'd ever seen. As he incrementally threw the ball harder and faster, he lost control of it and it bounded off the 20th floor balcony. To Carlos's surprise, there went Fido right after it! When Maria returned dressed and ready for dinner, she asked Carlos how he liked her dog. Almost without hesitation Carlos said, "I don't know about you, but Fido seemed a little depressed to me!"

As luck would have it, Fido landed on the awning of Maria's neighbor on the floor below and was returned uninjured. Still, one cannot help but be impressed with Carlos's ingenuity in the face of what he thought to be a hopeless situation. As you found out in the previous section of this workbook, there are many ways to cope with stressful occurrences. Would you have been able to manage the stress Carlos experienced? What do you typically do when finding yourself in a stressful situation? It is not enough to know about stress management techniques. You need to employ them to derive their benefits. Do you use effective management techniques often enough?

Scale 3.1: How Often Do You Use Techniques That Are Helpful in Managing Stress?

There are a number of techniques that have been shown to be effective in managing stress. The following scale measures how often you use such techniques.

> Listed on the following page are things that people sometimes do to manage stress. Think back over the past *month*. Place a check (✓) to show how often, during the past month, you have done each thing.

During the past month, how often did you . . .

	REGULARLY	OCCASIONALLY	RARELY
1. . . . get plenty of rest at night?			✓
2. . . . talk about your feelings with friends or family members?			✓
3. . . . take breaks when doing difficult tasks?		✓	
4. . . . drink less than three cups of coffee per day?	✓		
5. . . . plan your time so that you could meet all your responsibilities?		✓	
6. . . . use relaxation techniques?			✓
7. . . . ask others for help when you felt you had too much to do?			✓
8. . . . exercise?		✓	
9. . . . talk about your problems with the people who were involved in them?			✓
10. . . . figure out whether or not you were feeling stress?	✓		
11. . . . find interesting things to do when you were bored?		✓	
12. . . . plan time for relaxation?			✓
13. . . . look at the positive things in your life?		✓	
14. . . . say "no" to helping others when you felt you already had enough to do?		✓	
15. . . . set realistic goals for yourself?			✓

SCORING*

Assign the following point values for each response:

Regularly   = 3
Occasionally = 2
Rarely   = 1

Next, add the points and divide by 15.

INTERPRETATION OF SCORES

This is a scale that measures your use of a variety of stress management techniques. The maximum score obtainable of 3 indicates you frequently use a variety of stress management techniques, a score of 2 indicates you occasionally use stress management techniques, and a score of 1 indicates you rarely use stress management techniques. Any score below 2 means you need to employ methods to manage stress on a more regular basis.

As you can see from the checklist itself, there are plenty of things you can do to manage stress better. First and foremost is that you must take care of your health. That means you need to get enough sleep, eat well, refrain from using drugs, and exercise regularly. Do you do these?

It also helps to talk about your problems (stressors) with other people whose opinions you trust and with whom you feel comfortable sharing these concerns. Do you have friends or relatives with whom you do this now?

And do not forget the value in organizing your time so you do not feel overly pressured, taking breaks from stressful work every so often, finding interesting things to do as a diversion from your daily routine, focusing on the positive aspects of events rather than negative ones, and establishing realistic goals so you are not frustrated by attempting to accomplish goals that are unobtainable. Are these consistent with your actions now?

If you find these recommendations foreign to you, perhaps you need to spend some time rearranging your behaviors and thoughts. The activity section that follows will help, but if you are serious, you will need to either consult with your instructor and/or read a stress management book and/or enroll in a stress management workshop.

---

*Source: Centers for Disease Control. *An Evaluation Handbook for Health Education Programs in Stress Management.* Washington, DC: Department of Health and Human Services, 1983, pp. 76–79.

ACTIVITY: CHOOSING TECHNIQUES THAT WORK FOR YOU

The *Stress Management Checklist* you just completed includes numerous ways that have been found to be effective in managing stress. Review this list and identify those you think have the most relevance to you. That is, which of these techniques do you think are feasible for you to employ given your lifestyle, interests, and needs? Now place that list aside. You will come back to it shortly.

There are many other ways that people have found to manage stress. So as not to be limited in your options, interview at least three other people who, in your opinion, seem to have the stress of their lives under control. Ask them the following questions:

1. How do you manage the stress you experience?
2. What do you do to relax?
3. How do you look at stressful events so as to make them less stressful?
4. Who helps you manage the stress of your life?
5. Knowing me, what do you suggest I do to manage the stress that I experience?

From the answers you obtain to these questions, add to your list of stress management strategies. Now that your list is more complete, choose several (at least three) stress management techniques you will try. Remember that you are not wedded to any particular technique. If it is not working, try another. With some effort you will be able to manage the stress of your life. Don't give up.

Which three techniques will you try first?

1. _____

2. _____

3. _____

Section IV Life Situation Intervention: Life Satisfaction

So far we have inquired about your typical response to stress, what you know about stress and how to cope with it, and which stress management techniques you typically use. One of the most motivating influences on whether people will employ stress management techniques is how satisfied they are with their lives. Can you imagine anything more stressful than not being satisfied with your existence as it is? Some of you may even know people, or know someone who knows people, who have been so dissatisfied with their lives that they think about or actually attempt suicide. Obviously, this permanent solution is no solution at all. It not only ends the person's life but creates long-lasting distress and unhappiness (to say the least) in the lives of friends and relatives.

How satisfied are you with your life? Although you may not be seriously disillusioned, perhaps you are dissatisfied enough to begin employing stress management techniques regularly. The scale below will help you make that determination.

Scale 4.1: How Satisfied Are You with Your Overall Life?

How you feel about the satisfaction you derive from your life affects the degree of stress you experience. This scale measures your general level of satisfaction with your life.

Listed on the following page are several factors that might influence your overall life satisfaction. In the Importance column, indicate how important each factor is to you by using the following scale:

1 = Unimportant
2 = Somewhat important
3 = Very important

In the Satisfaction column, indicate how satisfied you are with each factor by using the following scale:

1 = Unsatisfied
2 = Somewhat satisfied
3 = Very satisfied

	FACTOR	IMPORTANCE	SATISFACTION
Your health			
Your physical appearance			
Your occupation (e.g., job, school, homemaking, child raising)			
Your ability to deal with people			
Your relationships with friends			
Your relationships with family			
Your sexual relationships			
Your spiritual life			
Your ability to handle problems			
Your financial condition			
Your leisure activities (e.g., hobbies, volunteer work, exercise program)			
Your accomplishments			
Your overall adjustment to life			

SCORING*

Multiply the point value you assigned for each factor on the "Satisfaction" rating by the point value you assigned for its corresponding "Importance" rating. This gives you a "weighted rating." Next, add the point values of all the weighted ratings and divide this sum by the average "Importance" rating in all factors. The weighted "Satisfaction" score is computed by dividing this number by the number of weighted responses (13). The maximum score is 3.0.

INTERPRETATION OF SCORES

This scale measures how satisfied you are with your life. High scores indicate a high degree of life satisfaction, giving more weight to those factors you consider to be the most important.

---

*Source: Centers for Disease Control. *An Evaluation Handbook for Health Education Programs in Stress Management.* Washington, DC: Department of Health and Human Services, 1983, pp. 83–85.

In viewing the results of this scale, focus on those aspects of your overall life that you think are most important. Realize that, in fact, you may be making the wrong judgment here. For example, if you rate your physical appearance as more important than your health, you might be tempted to use anabolic steroids to look good. Unfortunately, these drugs can make you look good as a corpse! Short of that, they can make males impotent and encourage the growth of facial hair in females, among other serious and disturbing effects. And yet, unless it is important to you, it is unlikely you will devote the time and energy to work on improving that aspect of your life. Therefore, it makes sense to focus on that which you believe to be important. If you are successful at improving that aspect of your life, you will feel more confident and, as a result, less distressed.

In the case that an aspect of your life cannot be improved, there are probably things you can do to be more accepting of it. For example, you may dislike your big nose thinking it takes up about 50 percent more of your face than you would like. Well, you might not be willing to have it operated on, but you could hang out with people whose noses are *really* big. Then, your nose, relatively speaking, will appear to be more reasonably sized.

On a more serious note, you may not be able to nor want to improve your relationship with a family member. Perhaps you were abused by this person when younger. What you can do, though, is arrange for counseling so you can more easily accept that this relationship will remain distant. Counseling may help you see the abuse as a significant event in your life, but one that happened long ago. Then you might be better able to be successful, develop other meaningful relationships, and be more satisfied with your life.

ACTIVITY: FOCUS GROUPING

Once you have identified those general aspects of your life that you wish to improve, seek the help and advice of people whose opinions you respect—maybe friends, relatives, teachers, clergy. One way to do this is to organize a focus group. Focus groups have a specific topic to discuss and are guided through this discussion by questions posed to them by the focus group leader (in this case, you). The first step is for you to develop a "focus group guide" that includes specific questions you want the group to answer, in the order in which you want them discussed. Then, ask people whose advice you think would be valuable to meet at a specific time and place for a specified period of time—Monday, February 21st, in my apartment, from 6:30 p.m. until 8:00 p.m. You might want to provide snacks to make the group feel comfortable. Make sure you take good notes and/or tape record the group discussion.

One very important point that needs emphasizing is that you should not influence the advice you get from the focus group members. You should merely throw out a question, rather than make a suggestion and ask the group what they think of it. Do not react to any suggestions the group offers and do not become defensive about what you hear. You do not want to stifle any suggestions that have value. You can always react after the group has finished its discussion and, at that point, discount any suggestions you judge to be nonsensical.

Scale 4.2: How Satisfied Are You with Particular Facets of Your Life?

To obtain a measure more specific to particular facets of your life and your satisfaction with them, complete the scale below.

> Consider how things have been going for you during the last few weeks. Below is a list of things that can influence your happiness and satisfaction with life. Please read each item and indicate how you have felt about it over the last few weeks. Indicate whether you have felt terrible, unhappy, mostly dissatisfied, mixed, mostly satisfied, pleased, or delighted. Circle one answer for each.

Over the last few weeks, how have you felt about . . .	TERRIBLE	UNHAPPY	MOSTLY DISSATISFIED	MIXED	MOSTLY SATISFIED	PLEASED	DELIGHTED
1. . . . your overall satisfaction with your work (including being a student or homemaker)?	1	2	3	4	5	6	7
2. . . . the amount of income you have?	1	2	3	4	5	6	7
3. . . . the amount of pay you get for the amount of work you do?	1	2	3	4	5	6	7
4. . . . your liking for the actual work itself that is involved in your job?	1	2	3	4	5	6	7
5. . . . the physical surroundings and working conditions in your job?	1	2	3	4	5	6	7

	TERRIBLE	UNHAPPY	MOSTLY DISSATISFIED	MIXED	MOSTLY SATISFIED	PLEASED	DELIGHTED
6. . . . the amount of job security you have?	1	2	3	4	5	6	7
7. . . . your overall health?	1	2	3	4	5	6	7
8. . . . your overall physical condition?	1	2	3	4	5	6	7
9. . . . the amount of time you have for doing things you want to do?	1	2	3	4	5	6	7
10. . . . the chances you have for recreation and just taking it easy?	1	2	3	4	5	6	7
11. . . . what you are accomplishing with your life?	1	2	3	4	5	6	7
12. . . . your ability to change things around you that you don't like?	1	2	3	4	5	6	7
13. . . . how interesting your day-to-day life is?	1	2	3	4	5	6	7
14. . . . your ability to satisfy and meet your needs?	1	2	3	4	5	6	7
15. . . . the fullness and completeness of your love/sex life?	1	2	3	4	5	6	7
16. . . . your ability to handle your emotions and feelings?	1	2	3	4	5	6	7

	TERRIBLE	UNHAPPY	MOSTLY DISSATISFIED	MIXED	MOSTLY SATISFIED	PLEASED	DELIGHTED
17. . . . your religious life?	1	2	3	4	5	6	7
18. . . . the enjoyment you experience when you are around other people?	1	2	3	4	5	6	7
19. . . . how honest and sincere other people are with you?	1	2	3	4	5	6	7
20. . . . your ability to gain cooperation from other persons?	1	2	3	4	5	6	7
21. . . . your general enjoyment of life?	1	2	3	4	5	6	7
22. . . . your sensitivity to other persons' feelings?	1	2	3	4	5	6	7
23. . . . your standard of living: the things you have such as housing, car, furniture, recreation, etc.?	1	2	3	4	5	6	7
24. . . . how consistent and understandable your world seems to be?	1	2	3	4	5	6	7
25. . . . the degree of love and acceptance you feel from others?	1	2	3	4	5	6	7
26. . . . how happy you are?	1	2	3	4	5	6	7

	TERRIBLE	UNHAPPY	MOSTLY DISSATISFIED	MIXED	MOSTLY SATISFIED	PLEASED	DELIGHTED
27. ... your independence and freedom: the chance to do what you want to do?	1	2	3	4	5	6	7
28. ... how you have handled problems that have come up?	1	2	3	4	5	6	7
29. ... how much fun you are having?	1	2	3	4	5	6	7
30. ... your ability to take it when things get tough?	1	2	3	4	5	6	7
31. ... the amount of intimacy and warmth in your life?	1	2	3	4	5	6	7
32. ... the respect you get from others?	1	2	3	4	5	6	7
33. ... your ability to adjust to changes that come along?	1	2	3	4	5	6	7
34. ... your ability to get along with other people?	1	2	3	4	5	6	7
35. ... the amount of friendship and love in your life?	1	2	3	4	5	6	7
36. ... your own family life?	1	2	3	4	5	6	7
37. ... your close relatives: parents, brothers, sisters, in-laws, etc.?	1	2	3	4	5	6	7

	TERRIBLE	UNHAPPY	MOSTLY DISSATISFIED	MIXED	MOSTLY SATISFIED	PLEASED	DELIGHTED
38. . . . the things you do and the times you have with friends?	1	2	3	4	5	6	7
39. . . . the standards and values in today's society?	1	2	3	4	5	6	7
40. . . . your prospects for a good life in the future?	1	2	3	4	5	6	7
41. . . . your success in getting ahead in the world?	1	2	3	4	5	6	7
42. . . . your ability to concentrate?	1	2	3	4	5	6	7
43. . . . your ability to get things done efficiently?	1	2	3	4	5	6	7
44. . . . your ability to express your ideas to others?	1	2	3	4	5	6	7
45. . . . your ability to share your feelings with persons who are close to you?	1	2	3	4	5	6	7
46. . . . your ability to think things through and come up with good answers?	1	2	3	4	5	6	7

SCORING*

Add up your circled responses and divide by 46.

INTERPRETATION OF SCORES

This scale measures how satisfied you are with various facets of your life. High scores indicate a high degree of satisfaction. If you scored lower than 4.0, you indicated dissatisfaction with various facets of your life. If you scored above 4.0, you indicated satisfaction with many aspects of your life. Look at those items for which you responded with a 3 or less. Those are the facets of your life with which you are particularly dissatisfied.

No one of us can be expected to be satisfied with every particular facet of our lives. In interpreting your scores, you probably found some areas of your life about which you feel pleased or delighted and others about which you feel unhappy or terrible. That is quite natural. What is unfortunate is that some people feel stymied by their shortcomings and let them interfere with finding satisfaction and fulfillment. There is always something that can be done to either improve a facet of your life so you are less dissatisfied with it or employ some strategies to feel better about those facets of your life that cannot be changed. We discussed this in relation to the previous scale.

So, rather than bemoan facets of your life for which you scored low, let's do something about them. The activity that follows presents one way to do that.

ACTIVITY: MAKING A CONTRACT

Check the items on the *NIDA Life Satisfaction Questionnaire* to which you responded with a 1 or 2; that is, those items about which you feel either "Terrible" or "Unhappy." These are the items you need to work on changing if you expect to be more satisfied with your life. A good way to begin is to develop a contract with yourself, witnessed by someone else who you think will be supportive, to make the necessary change. You can use the contract that is below.

First you need to consider appropriate rewards for being able to successfully make the change you will soon identify. List these now:

REWARDS

1. _____

2. _____

3. _____

4. _____

5. _____

---

*Source: U.S. Department of Health and Human Services and National Institute on Drug Abuse. Research Issue 28. *Assessing Marijuana Consequences: Selected Questionnaire Items*. DHHS Publication No. (ADM) 81-1150. Washington, DC: U.S. Government Printing Office, 1981.

Next, identify a supportive person you think can help you to make this change. Then complete this contract:

CONTRACT

I _____ desire to improve _____ because
         (your name)

_____ . I have
         (the reason)

decided I intend to _____ by
         (your target behavior)

_____ . If I achieve this goal, I will reward myself by _____ .
  (date)   (the reward)

_____   _____
(Your signature)   (Today's date)

_____   _____
(Witness signature)   (Today's date)

Researchers have found contracts to be very effective in helping people make changes. You, too, can be successful and your life, thereby, more satisfying.

Scale 4.3: How Optimistic Are You About Your Future?

Feeling satisfied with your life at present is certainly important, but it is also important to maintain a positive outlook on your future in order to be satisfied and happy. Without such an outlook, you may experience a great deal of stress from everyday hassles, as well as extraordinary events, that will be extremely stressful and unmanageable. Optimism will go a long way to help you cope with the stress of your life. Feeling positive about what the future holds can provide you with protection against the harmful effects of stress. It is vital to believe that although things may not be as you desire today, they can be better in the future. In this way, there will always be hope.

      The *Life Satisfaction Inventory* you completed earlier sought to determine how satisfied with your life you are at present. The *How Will You Feel?* scale presented on the following pages, although similar to the *Life Satisfaction Inventory,* measures your outlook (your optimism) by asking you to guess at the life satisfaction you will experience in the short term (one year) and in the long term (10 years).

Listed on the following page are several factors that might influence your expectations about the quality of your life in the near and distant future.

In the Importance column, indicate how important each factor is to you by using the following scale:

> 1 = Unimportant
> 2 = Somewhat important
> 3 = Very important

In the Expected Satisfaction in One Year column, indicate how satisfied you expect to be with each factor *one year from now.*

In the Expected Satisfaction in Ten Years column, indicate how satisfied you expect to be with each factor *ten years from now.*

For both Expected Satisfaction columns, use the following scale:

> 1 = Expect to be *unsatisfied*
> 2 = Expect to be *somewhat satisfied*
> 3 = Expect to be *very satisfied*

FACTOR	IMPORTANCE	EXPECTED SATISFACTION IN ONE YEAR	EXPECTED SATISFACTION IN TEN YEARS
Your health			
Your physical appearance			
Your occupation (e.g., job, school, homemaking, child raising)			
Your ability to deal with people			
Your relationships with friends			
Your relationships with family			
Your sexual relationships			
Your spiritual life			
Your ability to handle problems			
Your financial condition			
Your leisure activities (e.g., hobbies, volunteer work, exercise program)			
Your accomplishments			
Your overall adjustment to life			

SCORING*

Add the point values in the "Importance" column to determine your "Importance Rating." Then add the point values in each of the "Expected Satisfaction" columns to determine your "Expected Satisfaction Ratings." Next, divide each of the "Expected Satisfaction Ratings" by the "Importance Rating" score to determine your "Importance-Weighted Expected Satisfaction" score for one year and ten years. For either the one- or ten-year period, the maximum score attainable is 3.0.

Separate scores for each time period also can be combined to obtain an "Overall Importance-Weighted Satisfaction Score." To obtain this score, add the "Importance-Weighted Expected Satisfaction" scores for the 1-year and 10-year periods and then divide that sum by 2. The maximum "Overall Importance-Weighted Expected Satisfaction" score attainable is 3.0.

* *Source:* Centers for Disease Control. *An Evaluation Handbook for Health Education Programs in Stress Management.* Washington, DC: Department of Health and Human Services, 1983, pp. 183–186.

INTERPRETATION OF SCORES

This scale measures how optimistic you are about your future life satisfaction for two time periods: one year from now and 10 years from now. High scores for the separate time periods or their combination indicate highly optimistic expectations for life satisfaction, giving more weight to those factors considered by you to be most important. If your scores are below 2.0, that indicates you are not optimistic that your future will be sufficiently satisfying for you.

Stress management teaches you to be more in control of yourself and your life than you thought you could. That control may relate to being in charge of your thoughts and feelings such as anxiety and depression, your physiology such as the degree of muscle tension or how fast your heart beats, or the closeness and meaningfulness of your personal relationships. Stress management also strives to put you in control of the satisfaction you derive from life. If you find you are pessimistic about your future, do something about that now. For example, if you are concerned about your occupational future—what kind of a job you will have and how much money you will make—you can always prepare yourself now by learning a skill that will be marketable in the future. If you are concerned about being effective and happy socially—finding someone who will love you and developing friendships that will be long-lasting—you can enroll in workshops or courses that study skills related to communication, conflict resolution, assertiveness, and the like.

You need not be a ship, rudderless on the high seas, tossed here and there at whim. You can steer toward the future you desire as long as your goals are realistic. But that may mean preparing now rather than waiting for a turn for the worse during which you bemoan your situation.

I'm reminded of the town that had a problem with people falling over a cliff. Some townspeople argued for putting an ambulance in the valley to help those who fell over. Others fought for the construction of a fence to prevent people from falling over the cliff in the first place. What will you do with your life? Place an ambulance in your valley, or build a fence to take charge from the beginning? If you decide prevention is the better course, the activity that follows will be a good beginning.

ACTIVITY: PEOPLE/PLACES GRID

You have more control over your future than you might think. You can arrange your life to be more satisfying if you exercise that control. For example, you can spend time with people that you enjoy being with and can hang out at places where you derive satisfaction. Then, you will be more optimistic about your short-range and long-range future. The following activity will help you organize your life to do that.

Fill in the following *People/Places Grid*. In Quadrant I, list five people you like; in Quadrant II, list five people you dislike; in Quadrant III, list five places you like; and in Quadrant IV, list five places you dislike.

PEOPLE/PLACES GRID

People Liked:	People Disliked:
1. 2. 3. 4. 5. I	II 1. 2. 3. 4. 5.
III Places Liked: 1. 2. 3. 4. 5.	IV Places Disliked: 1. 2. 3. 4. 5.

Now, on a separate sheet of paper, you are going to identify the characteristics of people you like and dislike and places you like and dislike.

Take Quadrant I first: What do the people that you like have in common? Perhaps they have a good sense of humor or are caring and considerate. Perhaps they enjoy sports or are hard workers. On your separate sheet of paper, list these characteristics. Don't limit yourself to characteristics that *all* of them possess, but rather characteristics that describe *many* (at least three of the five) people you've listed.

Let's look at Quadrant II now: What do the people that you dislike have in common? Perhaps they are noisy or are poor listeners. Perhaps they are too serious or are selfish. On your separate sheet of paper, list these characteristics. Again, don't limit yourself to characteristics that *all* of them possess, but rather characteristics that describe at least three of the five people you've listed.

We'll do the same for Quadrant III: What is it that places you like have in common? Perhaps they are busy and noisy or all full of activity. Perhaps they are quiet and conducive to conversation. Perhaps they have warm climates or an ocean or other body of water nearby. On your separate sheet of paper, list these characteristics. Again, don't limit yourself to characteristics that *all* of them possess, but rather characteristics that describe at least three of the five places you've listed.

Lastly, do the same for Quadrant IV: What is it that places you dislike have in common? Perhaps they are too quiet or lack interesting things to do. Perhaps they are in cold, windy climates or too remote from a large city. Perhaps they are too "high brow" and not "earthy" enough for you. Once again, don't limit yourself to characteristics that *all* of them possess, but rather characteristics that describe at least three of the five places you've listed.

Now that you've identified characteristics descriptive of people and places you like and dislike, you can use this information to make your life more satisfying and less stressful. For instance, make a plan to spend time with the *kind of people* you like and limit relationships with the *kind of people* you dislike. This seems obvious. However, we don't always use this strategy when meeting new people, and don't really understand why it is that other relationships of ours are either so enjoyable or so unpleasant.

Increase the likelihood of being more satisfied with your life and less stressful by filling in the information below.

PEOPLE AND PLACES ANALYSIS

Who are the people you want to spend more time with?

_____   _____

_____   _____

_____   _____

Who are the people you want to limit time with?

_____   _____

_____   _____

_____   _____

Where do you want to spend more time?

_____   _____

_____   _____

_____   _____

Where do you want to limit time?

_____   _____

_____   _____

_____   _____

There are other ways to use the information you've generated about the people and places you like and dislike. For instance, ask yourself the following questions:

1. What would happen if I took the people I like to the places I like?

   Would I have a *great* time? Or would I be unable to focus my attention on the people because of the characteristics of the place? Or would I be unable to focus my attention on the place because of the characteristics of the people?

2. What would happen if I took the people I like to the places I dislike?

   Would I like the people less? Or would I like the places more? Would the places interfere with my relationships with the people, or would the people be so enjoyable to be with that the negative characteristics of the places would be more tolerable?

3. What would happen if I took the people I dislike to the places I like?

   Would I like the people more? Or would I like the places less because of sharing them with people around whom I feel uncomfortable? Could I ever enjoy these places again, or would they be forever ruined by the memory of having shared them with people I dislike? How would I feel if people I like found out I shared the places I like with people I dislike?

In essence, you have just asked yourself whether you are a *people* person or a *places* person. Are people more important to you than where you are, or is your environment more important to you than the people in it? There is no right or wrong answer. People just differ in this perspective. The point is that you should know which you find more important so you can better organize your life to be consistent with this perspective.

Scale 4.4: How Well Can You Read Food Labels?

In order to eat healthfully, you need to determine the various nutritional components in foods you are considering eating. Some foods may be "fat free" but may still be high-calorie foods. Conversely, some foods may be low-calorie foods but still not be "fat free." Some foods may provide the vitamins and minerals recommended for people experiencing a good deal of stress. Others may not. Because of their makeup, some foods may contribute to stress-related illnesses and diseases such as coronary heart disease, stroke, and hypertension. On the other hand, some foods may provide protection from these conditions.

The *How Well Can You Read Food Labels?* scale is designed to test your ability to make wise nutritional decisions by reading food labels.

Answer each of the following questions after reading the food labels provided. Answers are given following the five questions.

1. Increasing fiber in your diet is very important to you. Which of the muffins described below would you choose to maximize your fiber intake, the oat bran or the honey wheat muffins? Make your decision based on the food labels for each type of muffin.

Oat Bran Muffins

Nutrition Facts

Serving Size 1 muffin
Servings Per Container 2

Amount Per Serving	
Calories 250 Calories from Fat 110	
	% Daily Value*
Total Fat 12g	**18%**
Saturated Fat 3g	**15%**
Cholesterol 30mg	**10%**
Sodium 470mg	**20%**
Total Carbohydrate 31g	**10%**
Dietary Fiber 2g	**8%**
Sugars 5g	
Protein 5g	

Vitamin A 4%	•	Vitamin C 2%
Calcium 20%	•	Iron 4%

*Percent Daily Values are based on a 2,000 calorie diet. Your daily values may be higher or lower depending on your calorie needs:

		Calories:	2,000	2,500
Total Fat	Less than		65g	80g
Sat Fat	Less than		20g	25g
Cholesterol	Less than		300mg	300mg
Sodium	Less than		2,400mg	2,400mg
Total Carbohydrate			300g	375g
Dietary Fiber			25g	30g

Honey Wheat Muffins

Nutrition Facts

Serving Size 1 muffin
Servings Per Container 2

Amount Per Serving	
Calories 250 Calories from Fat 110	
	% Daily Value*
Total Fat 12g	**18%**
Saturated Fat 3g	**15%**
Cholesterol 30mg	**10%**
Sodium 470mg	**20%**
Total Carbohydrate 31g	**10%**
Dietary Fiber 3g	**12%**
Sugars 5g	
Protein 5g	

Vitamin A 4%	•	Vitamin C 2%
Calcium 20%	•	Iron 4%

*Percent Daily Values are based on a 2,000 calorie diet. Your daily values may be higher or lower depending on your calorie needs:

		Calories:	2,000	2,500
Total Fat	Less than		65g	80g
Sat Fat	Less than		20g	25g
Cholesterol	Less than		300mg	300mg
Sodium	Less than		2,400mg	2,400mg
Total Carbohydrate			300g	375g
Dietary Fiber			25g	30g

2.   *True or False?* These pretzels are low in sodium.

Nutrition Facts		
Serving Size 1 pretzel (about 25g)		
Servings Per Container 20		
Amount Per Serving		
Calories 90	Calories from Fat 0	
		% Daily Value*
Total Fat 0g		0%
Saturated Fat 0g		0%
Cholesterol 0mg		0%
Sodium 470mg		20%
Total Carbohydrate 19g		6%
Dietary Fiber less than 1g		4%
Sugars less than 1g		
Protein 1g		
Vitamin A *	Vitamin C *	
Calcium *	Iron *	
*Contains less than 2% of the Daily Value of these nutrients.		
*Percent Daily Values are based on a 2,000 calorie diet. Your daily values may be higher or lower depending on your calorie needs:		

	Calories:	2,000	2,500
Total Fat	Less than	65g	80g
Sat Fat	Less than	20g	25g
Cholesterol	Less than	300mg	300mg
Sodium	Less than	2,400mg	2,400mg
Total Carbohydrate		300g	375g
Dietary Fiber		25g	30g

3. You love dessert, but you're concerned about your calorie intake. Which of these is lower in calories: half a container of the low-fat blueberry frozen yogurt or the whole container of low-fat cherry yogurt?

**Low-Fat
Blueberry Frozen Yogurt**

**Low-Fat
Cherry Yogurt**

Nutrition Facts
Serving Size 1/2 cup (98g)
Servings Per Container 4

Amount Per Serving

Calories 160 Calories from Fat 25

	% Daily Value*
Total Fat 2.5g	4%
Saturated Fat 1.5g	7%
Cholesterol 30mg	11%
Sodium 60mg	2%
Total Carbohydrate 26g	9%
Dietary Fiber less than 1g	4%
Sugars 18g	
Protein 8g	

Vitamin A 2%	•	Vitamin C 0%
Calcium 20%	•	Iron 4%

*Percent Daily Values are based on a 2,000 calorie diet. Your daily values may be higher or lower depending on your calorie needs:

	Calories:	2,000	2,500
Total Fat	Less than	65g	80g
Sat Fat	Less than	20g	25g
Cholesterol	Less than	300mg	300mg
Sodium	Less than	2,400mg	2,400mg
Total Carbohydrate		300g	375g
Dietary Fiber		25g	30g

Nutrition Facts
Serving Size 1 container (227g)
Servings Per Container 1

Amount Per Serving

Calories 250 Calories from Fat 20

	% Daily Value*
Total Fat 2.5g	4%
Saturated Fat 1.5g	8%
Cholesterol 15mg	5%
Sodium 110mg	5%
Total Carbohydrate 48g	16%
Dietary Fiber 0g	0%
Sugars 47g	
Protein 8g	

Vitamin A 0%	•	Vitamin C 0%
Calcium 30%	•	Iron 0%

*Percent Daily Values are based on a 2,000 calorie diet. Your daily values may be higher or lower depending on your calorie needs:

	Calories:	2,000	2,500
Total Fat	Less than	65g	80g
Sat Fat	Less than	20g	25g
Cholesterol	Less than	300mg	300mg
Sodium	Less than	2,400mg	2,400mg
Total Carbohydrate		300g	375g
Dietary Fiber		25g	30g

4. You are concerned about your calcium intake. Which has more calcium: *half* the container of the low-fat blueberry frozen yogurt or the *whole* container of the low-fat cherry yogurt?

Low-Fat Blueberry Frozen Yogurt

Nutrition Facts

Serving Size 1/2 cup (98g)
Servings Per Container 4

Amount Per Serving

Calories 160   Calories from Fat 25

	% Daily Value*
Total Fat 2.5g	4%
Saturated Fat 1.5g	7%
Cholesterol 30mg	11%
Sodium 60mg	2%
Total Carbohydrate 26g	9%
Dietary Fiber less than 1g	4%
Sugars 18g	
Protein 8g	

Vitamin A 2%	•	Vitamin C 0%
Calcium 20%	•	Iron 4%

*Percent Daily Values are based on a 2,000 calorie diet. Your daily values may be higher or lower depending on your calorie needs:

	Calories:	2,000	2,500
Total Fat	Less than	65g	80g
Sat Fat	Less than	20g	25g
Cholesterol	Less than	300mg	300mg
Sodium	Less than	2,400mg	2,400mg
Total Carbohydrate		300g	375g
Dietary Fiber		25g	30g

Low-Fat Cherry Yogurt

Nutrition Facts

Serving Size 1 container (227g)
Servings Per Container 1

Amount Per Serving

Calories 250   Calories from Fat 20

	% Daily Value*
Total Fat 2.5g	4%
Saturated Fat 1.5g	8%
Cholesterol 15mg	5%
Sodium 110mg	5%
Total Carbohydrate 48g	16%
Dietary Fiber 0g	0%
Sugars 47g	
Protein 8g	

Vitamin A 0%	•	Vitamin C 0%
Calcium 30%	•	Iron 0%

*Percent Daily Values are based on a 2,000 calorie diet. Your daily values may be higher or lower depending on your calorie needs:

	Calories:	2,000	2,500
Total Fat	Less than	65g	80g
Sat Fat	Less than	20g	25g
Cholesterol	Less than	300mg	300mg
Sodium	Less than	2,400mg	2,400mg
Total Carbohydrate		300g	375g
Dietary Fiber		25g	30g

5. To stay healthy, you want to limit the *total* amount of saturated fat you eat during the day. *True or False?* Any one of the following meals can be part of a healthy diet.

Four-Cheese Pizza

Nutrition Facts
Serving Size 1 Pizza (198g)
Servings Per Container 1

Amount Per Serving

Calories 530 Calories from Fat 240

	% Daily Value*
Total Fat 27g	**42%**
Saturated Fat 10g	**50%**
Cholesterol 50mg	**17%**
Sodium 1,090mg	**45%**
Total Carbohydrate 50g	**17%**
Dietary Fiber 4g	**17%**
Sugars 6g	
Protein 24g	

Vitamin A 35%	•	Vitamin C	0%
Calcium 50%	•	Iron	8%

*Percent Daily Values are based on a 2,000 calorie diet. Your daily values may be higher or lower depending on your calorie needs:

	Calories:	2,000	2,500
Total Fat	Less than	65g	80g
Sat Fat	Less than	20g	25g
Cholesterol	Less than	300mg	300mg
Sodium	Less than	2,400mg	2,400mg
Total Carbohydrate		300g	375g
Dietary Fiber		25g	30g

Macaroni and Cheese

Nutrition Facts
Serving Size 3.5 oz (98g)
Servings Per Container about 4

Amount Per Serving

Calories 320 Calories from Fat 90

	% Daily Value*
Total Fat 10g	**15%**
Saturated Fat 6g	**30%**
Cholesterol 25mg	**8%**
Sodium 730mg	**30%**
Total Carbohydrate 44g	**15%**
Dietary Fiber 1g	**4%**
Sugars 4g	
Protein 14g	

Vitamin A 10%	•	Vitamin C	0%
Calcium 20%	•	Iron	15%

*Percent Daily Values are based on a 2,000 calorie diet. Your daily values may be higher or lower depending on your calorie needs:

	Calories:	2,000	2,500
Total Fat	Less than	65g	80g
Sat Fat	Less than	20g	25g
Cholesterol	Less than	300mg	300mg
Sodium	Less than	2,400mg	2,400mg
Total Carbohydrate		300g	375g
Dietary Fiber		25g	30g

Deluxe Combo Pizza

Nutrition Facts
Serving Size 1 Pizza (186g)
Servings Per Container 1

Amount Per Serving

Calories 380 Calories from Fat 100

	% Daily Value*
Total Fat 11g	**17%**
Saturated Fat 3.5g	**18%**
Cholesterol 40mg	**13%**
Sodium 550mg	**23%**
Total Carbohydrate 47g	**16%**
Dietary Fiber 6g	**24%**
Sugars 4g	
Protein 23g	

Vitamin A 15%	•	Vitamin C	8%
Calcium 50%	•	Iron	20%

*Percent Daily Values are based on a 2,000 calorie diet. Your daily values may be higher or lower depending on your calorie needs:

	Calories:	2,000	2,500
Total Fat	Less than	65g	80g
Sat Fat	Less than	20g	25g
Cholesterol	Less than	300mg	300mg
Sodium	Less than	2,400mg	2,400mg
Total Carbohydrate		300g	375g
Dietary Fiber		25g	30g

SCORING*

1. One honey wheat muffin has more fiber than one oat bran muffin.
2. False. These pretzels are high in sodium.
3. The whole container of low-fat cherry yogurt has fewer calories than half a container of low-fat blueberry frozen yogurt.
4. Half the container (two servings) of low-fat blueberry frozen yogurt has more calcium than the whole container of low-fat cherry yogurt; 40 percent is more than 30 percent.
5. True. If you are careful, you can fit any of these meals into a healthful diet.

---

* *Source: Test Your Food Label Knowledge!* U.S. Food and Drug Administration Center for Food Safety and Applied Nutrition, Office of Nutritional Products, Labeling and Dietary Supplements. February 2002. http://www.cfsan.fda.gov/~dms/flquiz4a.html.

INTERPRETATION OF SCORES

1. Each oat bran muffin has only 2g of fiber (8 percent of the daily value); each honey wheat muffin has 3g of fiber (12 percent of the daily value). Note: To compare fiber, look at the Nutrition Facts panel and compare the % Daily Value of dietary fiber on each package.

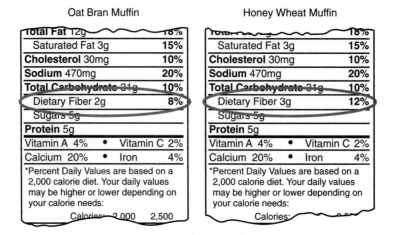

Oat Bran Muffin		Honey Wheat Muffin	

2. Use the % Daily Value as your guide for which foods are high or low in a nutrient. Quick guide to % Daily Value: 5 percent daily value or less is low; 20 percent daily value or more is high.

3. The whole container of low-fat cherry yogurt has fewer calories.

Blueberry Frozen Yogurt:
1/2 container = 2 servings
2 × 160 = 320 calories

Cherry Yogurt:
1 container = 1 serving
1 × 250 = 250 calories

Low-Fat Blueberry Frozen Yogurt   Low-Fat Cherry Yogurt

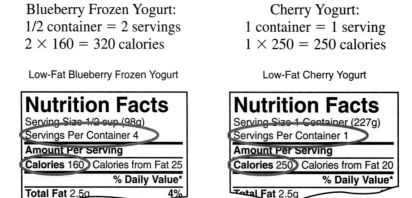

4. Half the container (2 servings) of low-fat blueberry frozen yogurt has more calcium: 40 percent is more than 30 percent!

Blueberry Frozen Yogurt:
1/2 container = 2 servings
2 × 20% = 40% daily value
for calcium

Cherry Yogurt:
1 container = 1 serving
1 × 30% = 30% daily value
for calcium

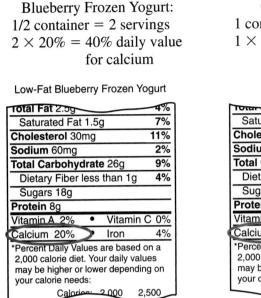

Low-Fat Blueberry Frozen Yogurt

Total Fat 2.5g	4%
Saturated Fat 1.5g	7%
Cholesterol 30mg	11%
Sodium 60mg	2%
Total Carbohydrate 26g	9%
Dietary Fiber less than 1g	4%
Sugars 18g	
Protein 8g	
Vitamin A 2% • Vitamin C 0%	
Calcium 20% • Iron 4%	

*Percent Daily Values are based on a 2,000 calorie diet. Your daily values may be higher or lower depending on your calorie needs:
Calories: 2,000   2,500

Low-Fat Cherry Yogurt

Total Fat	4%
Saturated Fat 1.5g	8%
Cholesterol 15mg	5%
Sodium 110mg	5%
Total Carbohydrate 48g	16%
Dietary Fiber 0g	0%
Sugars 47g	
Protein 8g	
Vitamin A 0% • Vitamin C 0%	
Calcium 30% • Iron 0%	

*Percent Daily Values are based on a 2,000 calorie diet. Your daily values may be higher or lower depending on your calorie needs:
Calories:

5. You can fit many different types of meals into a healthful diet if you pay careful attention to nutritional labeling

Four-Cheese Pizza: This choice is hardest to fit into a healthy diet. 1 serving (the whole pizza) uses 50 percent of your daily saturated fat allowance, leaving you only 50% for all other foods and drinks that day.

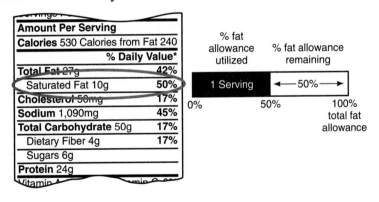

Amount Per Serving
Calories 530 Calories from Fat 240

	% Daily Value*
Total Fat 27g	42%
Saturated Fat 10g	50%
Cholesterol 50mg	17%
Sodium 1,090mg	45%
Total Carbohydrate 50g	17%
Dietary Fiber 4g	17%
Sugars 6g	
Protein 24g	

% fat allowance utilized   % fat allowance remaining

1 Serving ← 50% →

0%   50%   100%
total fat allowance

Macaroni and Cheese: This choice is not as hard to fit into a healthy diet. 1 serving uses 30 percent of your daily saturated fat allowance. This leaves you 70 percent for the rest of the day.

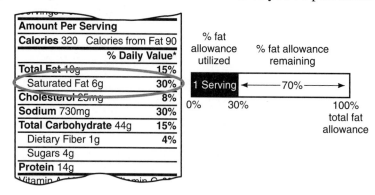

However, if you ate all four servings in the container (120 percent daily value for saturated fat), you would be well over your daily maximum of 100 percent!

Deluxe Combo Pizza: This meal is easiest to fit into a healthy diet. If you ate one serving (the whole pizza), you would consume 18 percent of your daily saturated fat allowance. This leaves you 82 percent of your saturated fat budget for all other foods eaten that day.

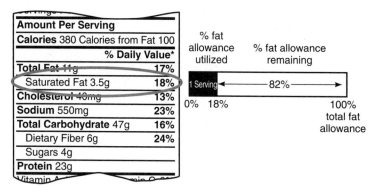

Note: A footnote on every nutrition label shows that the % Daily Values are based on a 2,000-calorie diet. If your calories needs are high, like young athletes, you will have a greater fat allowance. Also, it's important to check the Nutrition Facts panel of each product because the calories and % Daily Value for fat, or any nutrient, can vary greatly from product to product.

ACTIVITY: PLANNING FOR HEALTHY EATING

There are several steps you can take if you desire to adopt a healthy diet. These steps are outlined below:

Step 1: Inspect the foods you now have. For each packaged item, identify those foods that are unhealthy; for example, those too high in saturated fat, or that have too much sodium, or that are too high in calories. Once identified, these foods should be discarded. You can simply place them in the trash or, alternatively, donate them to a food pantry or homeless shelter.

Step 2: Plan a weekly menu that represents the recommended amount of calories, protein, carbohydrates, fats, vitamins, and minerals. Use the food pyramid guide as a reference for preparing the weekly menu. For guidance to make your diet specific to your culture, ethnicity, race, or food preferences, consult the sources below.

- *Food Guide Pyramid with a Mexican Flavor.*
  University of California Agriculture and Natural Resources. (800) 994-8849.
- *Puerto Rican Food Guide Pyramid.*
  Hispanic Health Council, the University of Connecticut Department of Nutrition, the COOP Extension, and the Connecticut State Department of Social Services.
- *East African Eating Guide for Good Health.*
  Native American Food Guide.
  Southeast Asian Food Guide.
  Pacific Northwest Native American Food Guide Brochure.
  Washington State Department of Health Warehouse Materials Management.
  (360) 664-9046 or fax, (360) 664-2929.
- *Multicultural Pyramid Packet* (cultural pyramids: African American, Chinese, Jewish, Puerto Rican, Navajo, Mexican, Indian, and Vietnamese).
  Penn State Nutrition Center, 5 Henderson Building, University Park, PA 16802.
  (814) 865-6323 or fax, (814) 865-5870.
- *Asian, Latin American, Mediterranean, and Vegetarian Food Pyramid Guides.* Oldways Preservation & Exchange Trust, 25 First Street, Cambridge, MA 02141. (617) 621-3000; fax, (617) 621-1230; http://www.oldways@tiac.net.

Step 3: Follow the weekly diet you prepared. At the end of the week, evaluate how well you adhered to the diet. If you notice you ate too much or too little of a particular nutrient, pay particular attention to not repeating that error the next week.

Step 4: Share your success with a friend or relative. Feeling proud of your newfound healthy eating lifestyle will encourage you to continue eating healthfully. And sharing that feeling of pride and success with someone whose opinions you value will further reinforce healthy eating.

Other Life Situation Interventions: Effective Communication Techniques

To use communication to help cope with stress, you need to know both how to communicate your feelings of stress to other people and how to communicate acceptance and understanding when other people share their stressful feelings with you. This section concerns these two communication skills.

Scale 5.1: How Well Can You Communicate Your Feelings of Stress to Other People?

Research shows that if you can share your feelings of stress with other people—loved ones, friends, relatives, co-workers, and classmates—you will be less apt to suffer from the negative effects of that stress. Just "venting" makes you feel that someone else cares—after all, these other people care enough about you to listen and attempt to recommend ways for you to feel better. Are you able to take advantage of this important resource? The scale that follows will help you determine how well you can communicate your feelings of stress to other people.

> This test presents descriptions of people who want to communicate their feelings about stress. They each have a message that they want to communicate to someone else.
>
> Read each item. Then circle the letter of the choice that expresses the individual's message clearly and directly. If there is no clear and direct response given, circle choice D, "None of the above."

1. Michael wants to communicate to his friend that he gets nervous while driving through heavy traffic. The most clear and direct way for Michael to say this is:
   A. "I get really anxious when I have to drive in heavy traffic."
   B. "Everyone who drives in heavy traffic gets nervous."
   C. "I can't possibly drive home through this traffic without getting nervous."
   D. None of the above.

2. Martin wants to tell his son that he feels depressed about retiring from the company where he has worked for twenty years. The most clear and direct way for Martin to say this is:
   A. "You know how I feel about not working anymore."
   B. "I'll be retiring from the company soon."
   C. "I feel sad when I realize I won't be going into work anymore."
   D. None of the above.

3. Reggie wants to ask his wife to serve herbal tea instead of coffee at night to help him relax. The most clear and direct way for Reggie to say this is:
    A. "People can't relax if they are served coffee at night."
    B. "You're not being very sensitive to my needs if you continue to serve coffee at night."
    C. "I think it would help me relax if you would serve herb tea after dinner."
    D. None of the above.

4. Joyce wants to tell her husband that she feels happy about being able to keep her cool during an important job interview. The most clear and direct way for Joyce to say this is:
    A. "Now I'll never have to worry again about getting nervous when I'm in a tight spot."
    B. "You know what it means to me to have remained calm during the interview."
    C. "I had a good job interview today."
    D. None of the above.

5. Mark wants to tell his friend that he gets anxious when he has to wait in long lines at the bank or in the grocery store. The most clear and direct way for Mark to say this is:
    A. "You know how annoyed I get when I'm stuck in a long line."
    B. "I am sure everybody hates waiting in long lines."
    C. "You must not have much to do if waiting in long lines doesn't bother you."
    D. None of the above.

6. Janice has started to meditate every evening to help her manage her stress more effectively. She wants to ask her roommate not to interrupt her when she's meditating. The most clear and direct way for Janice to say this is:
    A. "It's not very considerate of you to interrupt me when I'm meditating."
    B. "Please help me out by leaving me alone sometimes."
    C. "Please help me manage my stress by not interrupting me while I meditate."
    D. None of the above.

7. Bruce wants to tell James, his co-worker, that he feels good about being able to stay calm during a very busy time at the office. The most clear and direct way for Bruce to say this is:
    A. "I feel good about work now."
    B. "I was able to keep my cool during that busy time here and I feel good about it."
    C. "You know how good it feels to keep your cool during difficult times here in the office."
    D. None of the above.

8. Gerald plans to jog in the morning before work as part of his stress management program. He wants to ask his wife to help him by making sure he doesn't oversleep in the morning. The most clear and direct way for Gerald to say this is:
    A. "Everyone needs help sticking to a stress management program, so please help me with mine."
    B. "Please help me with my stress management program by making sure I get up on time to go jogging."
    C. "If you really care about my health, you'll help me get up on time to go jogging in the morning."
    D. None of the above.

9. Jane gets nervous driving to work in traffic. She decides to reduce her stress by riding her bicycle to work instead of taking the car. She wants to tell her friend that she feels good about her decision. The most clear and direct way for Jane to say this is:
   A. "Everyone should ride a bicycle to work."
   B. "I feel great about riding my bike instead of driving to work."
   C. "You can imagine how good I feel riding my bike to work."
   D. None of the above.

10. Valerie wants to tell her family that she's nervous about moving away to a different city. The most clear and direct way for Valerie to say this is:
    A. "There's no way I'll ever feel good about moving."
    B. "You couldn't possibly understand how I feel about moving."
    C. "I feel anxious about moving to another city."
    D. None of the above.

11. Gregg drinks a great deal of coffee at work and notices that it makes him feel nervous. He wants to ask his co-worker to help him drink less coffee by keeping track of the amount of coffee he drinks. The most clear and direct way for Gregg to say this is:
    A. "Please help me drink less coffee because you know how nervous I get when I drink too much coffee."
    B. "Either you're going to keep track of how much coffee I drink or I'm going to be a nervous wreck."
    C. "Please help me drink less coffee."
    D. None of the above.

12. Gwen is trying to reduce the stress in her life by setting up a weekly time schedule. She wants to tell her friend Henry that she's very happy about how much calmer she feels since she has started using the schedule. The most clear and direct way for Gwen to say this is:
    A. "You can see how much my time schedule has helped me."
    B. "I feel very calm since I've started setting up weekly time schedules."
    C. "I think everyone should use a weekly time schedule."
    D. None of the above.

13. Sheila is trying to consume less sugar as part of her stress management program. She wants to ask her roommate not to offer her anything sweet to eat. The most clear and direct way for Sheila to say this is:
    A. "Please don't offer me anything sweet because I'm trying to eat less sugar."
    B. "You don't help me when you offer me sweet foods to eat."
    C. "Everyone finds cutting back on sugar difficult, so please help me try to do it."
    D. None of the above.

14. Victor wants to tell his wife that he feels very nervous every time he thinks about the examination that he must take in a few weeks. The most clear and direct way for Victor to say this is:
    A. "This test that I have to take is a pain."
    B. "I guess I'll always get nervous about examinations."
    C. "You can imagine how nervous I am about the examination."
    D. None of the above.

15. Donald wants to tell his family how good he feels since he's started practicing progressive relaxation every day. The most clear and direct way for Donald to say this is:
 A. "You can tell how good I feel since I've started using progressive relaxation."
 B. "I feel great about practicing progressive relaxation every day."
 C. "You must be blind not to see how good I feel since I've started practicing relaxation."
 D. None of the above.

SCORING*

Assign yourself one point for each of the following responses:

1.	A	9.	B
2.	C	10.	C
3.	C	11.	D
4.	D	12.	B
5.	D	13.	A
6.	C	14.	D
7.	B	15.	B
8.	B		

A score over 10 indicates you communicate sufficiently well. However, we can all make improvements in how we interact with others. More important than your score is to understand the interpretation below.

INTERPRETATION OF SCORES

This scale measures how well you can communicate your feelings of stress to other people. Using the key below, you can evaluate your incorrect answers as being either

1. *Overgeneralized*—a response that extends a single experience to all experiences or always associates a particular behavior with certain circumstances.
2. *Crystal Ball*—a response in which the assumption is made that the receiver already knows the sender's feelings or the content of the message.
3. *Judgment*—a response that blames or criticizes.
4. *Incomplete*—a response that does not provide all the information needed to send a complete message.
5. *None of the Above*—a response that indicates there is no correct answer when there is a correct answer.

Source: Centers for Disease Control. *An Evaluation Handbook for Health Education Programs in Stress Management.* Washington, DC: Department of Health and Human Services, 1983, pp. 160–168.

	Overgeneralized	Crystal Ball	Judgment	Incomplete	None of the Above
1.	B,C	—	—	—	D
2.	—	A	—	B	D
3.	A	—	B	—	D
4.	A	B	—	C	—
5.	B	A	C	—	—
6.	—	—	A	B	D
7.	—	C	—	A	D
8.	A	—	C	—	D
9.	A	C	—	—	D
10.	A	—	B	—	D
11.	B	A	—	C	—
12.	C	A	—	—	D
13.	C	—	B	—	D
14.	B	C	—	A	—
15.	—	A	C	—	D

Different people communicate using different styles. Some of us are fortunate in that we somehow learned how to communicate effectively and do so. Others of us are deficient in our communication style and need to work to improve it. As I've said before, stress management is putting you in more control of you than you thought possible. Specific to our discussion here, you need to even take charge of how you communicate. If you cannot interact well with people, and that interferes with sharing your stressful feelings with them, you will not be as effective in managing stress as you might otherwise. The activity that follows should help begin the process of improving how you communicate with others about your stressful feelings.

ACTIVITY: CHANGING YOUR STYLE OF COMMUNICATING

Determine which type(s) of incorrect responses are typical of your style of communicating. Do you tend to overgeneralize, assume the other person already knows your feelings, make judgments that blame or criticize others, or convey incomplete messages? Perhaps you even employ more than one of these. Below are the items from the *Communicating About Stress* scale. Without referring back to the various options provided earlier, write a clear and direct response. When you are done, refer back to the correct choices as identified in the Scoring section and see if your written statements are comparable. Remember the style you identified as typical of your communication and try to avoid it.

1. Michael wants to communicate to his friend that he gets nervous while driving through traffic. The most clear and direct way for Michael to say this is:

    _____

    _____

    _____

2. Martin wants to tell his son that he feels depressed about retiring from the company where he has worked for twenty years. The most clear and direct way for Martin to say this is:

    _____

    _____

    _____

3. Reggie wants to ask his wife to serve herbal tea instead of coffee at night to help him relax. The most clear and direct way for Reggie to say this is:

    _____

    _____

    _____

4. Joyce wants to tell her husband that she feels happy about being able to keep her cool during an important job interview. The most clear and direct way for Joyce to say this is:

    _____

    _____

    _____

5. Mark wants to tell his friend that he gets anxious when he has to wait in long lines at the bank or in the grocery store. The most clear and direct way for Mark to say this is:

    _____

    _____

    _____

6.   Janice has started to meditate every evening to help her manage her stress more effectively. She wants to ask her roommate not to interrupt her when she's meditating. The most clear and direct way for Janice to say this is:

_____

_____

_____

7.   Bruce wants to tell James, his co-worker, that he feels good about being able to stay calm during a very busy time at the office. The most clear and direct way for Bruce to say this is:

_____

_____

_____

8.   Gerald plans to jog in the morning before work as part of his stress management program. He wants his wife to help him by making sure he doesn't oversleep in the morning. The most clear and direct way for Gerald to say this is:

_____

_____

_____

9.   Jane gets nervous driving to work in traffic. She decides to reduce her stress by riding her bicycle to work instead of taking the car. The most clear and direct way for Jane to say this is:

_____

_____

_____

10. Valerie wants to tell her family that she's nervous about moving away to a different city. The most clear and direct way for Valerie to say this is:

_____

_____

_____

11. Gregg drinks a great deal of coffee at work and notices that it makes him feel nervous. He wants to ask his co-worker to help him drink less coffee by keeping track of the amount of coffee he drinks. The most clear and direct way for Gregg to say this is:

_____

_____

_____

12. Gwen is trying to reduce the stress in her life by setting up a weekly time schedule. She wants to tell her friend Henry that she's very happy about how much calmer she feels since she started using the schedule. The most clear and direct way for Gwen to say this is:

_____

_____

_____

13. Sheila is trying to consume less sugar as part of her stress management program. She wants to ask her roommate not to offer her anything sweet to eat. The most clear and direct way for Sheila to say this is:

_____

_____

_____

14. Victor wants to tell his wife that he feels very nervous every time he thinks about the examination that he must take in a few weeks. The most clear and direct way for Victor to say this is:

_____

_____

_____

15. Donald wants to tell his family how good he feels since he started using progressive relaxation every day. The most clear and direct way for Donald to say this is:

_____

_____

_____

Scale 5.2: How Well Can You Communicate Acceptance and Understanding When Other People Share Their Stressful Feelings with You?

I conduct monthly stress management workshops for parents residing at the Ronald McDonald House in Washington, DC. These parents stay at the Ronald McDonald House while their seriously ill children are being treated in local hospitals. One part of the workshops focuses on the benefits of having others with whom to share problems, joys, and sorrows. Research is clear regarding the protection this type of social support provides against stress-related outcomes. Yet, whenever we get to this point in the workshop, the focus tends to be on how can I benefit from social support rather than how can I help others benefit from it. Workshop participants soon come to find out that the two are intertwined. Parents cannot receive support from others unless they are willing and able to give it back. No one wants to help or listen to someone else who is so tied into his or her own problems that he or she is unavailable to have others vent their frustrations to him or her. Realize, though, that being available is but the first step to offering support to others.

Part of learning to communicate about stress is to learn how to present yourself as accepting and understanding of other people's attempts at sharing their stressful feelings with you. If you can't express acceptance and understanding, how can you expect other people will express acceptance and understanding when you share your feelings of stress with them? This scale measures your skill in communicating acceptance and understanding when other people share their stressful feelings with you.

> This test presents statements by individuals who want to communicate their feelings about stress. Read each statement. Then circle the letter of the response that best communicates acceptance and understanding of the message.

1. Bonnie: "I get very anxious when I have to drive to work in heavy traffic." The response that best communicates acceptance and understanding of Bonnie's situation is:
   A. "Try to drive to work earlier in order to miss some of the traffic."
   B. "There really is no reason to get so anxious about driving in heavy traffic."
   C. "You become very nervous when you drive to work in heavy traffic."
   D. "You should take the bus to work instead of driving in heavy traffic."

2. Gary: "I feel very nervous at the office when I have more work to do than I can keep up with." The response that best communicates acceptance and understanding of Gary's situation is:
   A. "You will have a heart attack if you let yourself get so nervous."
   B. "It sounds like you're pushing yourself too hard at the office."
   C. "You never seem nervous at the office to me."
   D. "You feel nervous when you can't keep up with all the work you have to do at the office."

3.   Maggie: "I am proud of myself for practicing progressive relaxation every day."
     The response that best communicates acceptance and understanding of Maggie's situation is:
     A.   "You feel good about yourself because you're sticking to your progressive relaxation schedule."
     B.   "You'd sure be sorry if you didn't practice your relaxation skills every day."
     C.   "You should practice relaxation in the morning so you'll feel calm all day long."
     D.   "Try listening to soft music as you practice your relaxation skills."

4.   Mike: "I feel terrific because I've cut down on the amount of coffee I drink."
     The response that best communicates acceptance and understanding of Mike's situation is:
     A.   "You should drink herbal tea instead of whatever coffee you still drink."
     B.   "Drinking any coffee at all can make you very nervous."
     C.   "You're feeling great because you're drinking less coffee."
     D.   "If you still drink any coffee at all, that's too much."

5.   Fred: "Could you please not disturb me when I'm practicing my relaxation skills?"
     The response that best communicates acceptance and understanding of Fred's situation is:
     A.   "You should practice your relaxation skills when no one is around."
     B.   "You want me to leave you alone while you're practicing your relaxation?"
     C.   "Relaxation skills are useless if they don't work when there are distractions around."
     D.   "Try using ear plugs to block out noise while you are practicing."

6.   Francis: "I've been a little depressed since I moved away from my family."
     The response that best communicates acceptance and understanding of Francis's situation is:
     A.   "You're a little unhappy since you've left your family."
     B.   "Perhaps you were too attached to your family."
     C.   "You really have no reason to be depressed."
     D.   "Why don't you call your family every week to stay in touch with them?"

7.   Stuart: "I feel great about swimming three times a week as part of my stress management program."
     The response that best communicates acceptance and understanding of Stuart's situation is:
     A.   "Try swimming every day so that you'll feel even better."
     B.   "You'll be sorry if you don't stick to that stress management program."
     C.   "You don't need a stress management program."
     D.   "You're happy because you're swimming regularly as a part of your stress management program."

8.   Doug: "Would you help me manage my stress by encouraging me to make weekly time schedules?"
     The response that best communicates acceptance and understanding of Doug's situation is:
     A.   "You should rely on yourself only to manage your stress."
     B.   "You want me to encourage you to use time schedules to manage your stress?"
     C.   "You must doubt your ability to manage stress if you need my encouragement."
     D.   "You might be sorry if you depend on my encouragement to manage your stress."

9. Sara: "I've felt good since I started taking deep breaths whenever I am a little tense."
   The response that best communicates acceptance and understanding of Sara's situation is:
   A. "If you don't keep up deep breathing, you can end up just as nervous as you were."
   B. "Deep breaths help you relax and so probably they help you feel less stress."
   C. "You've started using deep breathing skills when you are tense and you feel good about that."
   D. "You might want to start exercising to help you reduce stress."

10. Matthew: "I'm really starting to enjoy the jogging that was prescribed as part of my stress management program."
    The response that best communicates acceptance and understanding of Matthew's situation is:
    A. "You're beginning to enjoy jogging now."
    B. "As the jogging gets easier for you, it also becomes more enjoyable."
    C. "Try jogging in the morning before you go to work."
    D. "You will have to continue to jog if you want to keep your stress level down."

11. Ellen: "Would you help me manage my stress by not offering me foods that contain a great deal of sugar?"
    The response that best communicates acceptance and understanding of Ellen's situation is:
    A. "You can eat some foods with sugar as long as you don't overdo it."
    B. "I'll be glad to help you, but you shouldn't need me to help you watch what you eat."
    C. "It must be very hard to avoid sugar when people frequently offer you sweet foods."
    D. "You want me to help you avoid foods with sugar by not offering you any?"

12. Ed: "I really feel anxious when I have to work in a noisy office."
    The response that best communicates acceptance and understanding of Ed's situation is:
    A. "There's no reason to let a little noise bother you."
    B. "Find the quietest area in the office and try to work there."
    C. "You get nervous when you have to work and the office is noisy."
    D. "Try to get used to the noise by taking deep breaths as soon as it starts to bother you."

13. Chris: "I feel a little embarrassed when I practice progressive relaxation at work."
    The response that best communicates acceptance and understanding of Chris's situation is:
    A. "I bet that you are worried about what your co-workers might think if they see you."
    B. "You're embarrassed when you practice your relaxation skills at work."
    C. "Think how nervous you'd feel if you didn't practice your relaxation skills at work."
    D. "Think of the good it does you instead of thinking about your embarrassment."

14. Julie: "I feel great because I'm changing my lifestyle to be simpler and less stressful."
    The response that best communicates acceptance and understanding of Julie's situation is:
    A. "I'm glad because you always had more things to do than you could do well."
    B. "You were headed for trouble if you didn't make your life less stressful."
    C. "You must have been under a lot of stress to make major changes in your lifestyle."
    D. "You are living a simpler, less stressful life and you feel good because of it."

15. Bill: "I'm proud that I've lowered my blood pressure by following a stress management program."
    The response that best communicates acceptance and understanding of Bill's situation is:
    A. "You should continue to follow your stress management program."
    B. "You're pleased that, because of following your stress management program, your blood pressure is lower."
    C. "You'll be sorry if you don't continue to follow your stress management program."
    D. "Your blood pressure wasn't that high in the first place."

SCORING*

Assign yourself one point for each of the following responses:

1.	C		9.	C
2.	D		10.	A
3.	A		11.	D
4.	C		12.	C
5.	B		13.	B
6.	A		14.	D
7.	D		15.	B
8.	B			

INTERPRETATION OF SCORES

This scale measures how well you can communicate acceptance and understanding when other people share their stressful feelings with you. Using the key below, you can evaluate your incorrect answers as being either

1. *Directing*—a response that tells or suggests to the message sender what to do.
2. *Warning*—a response that warns a message sender what might happen.
3. *Criticizing/Disagreeing*—a response that criticizes or disagrees with the message sender.
4. *Diagnosing*—a response that suggests an explanation for the message sender's statement.

Source: Centers for Disease Control. *An Evaluation Handbook for Health Education Programs in Stress Management.* Washington, DC: Department of Health and Human Services, 1983, pp. 174–182.

INCORRECT ANSWER CHOICE ANALYSIS

	Directing	Warning	Criticizing/Disagreeing	Diagnosing
1.	A,D	—	B	—
2.	—	A	C	B
3.	C,D	B	—	—
4.	A	B	D	—
5.	A,D	—	C	—
6.	D	—	C	B
7.	A	B	C	—
8.	A	D	—	C
9.	D	A	—	B
10.	C	D	—	B
11.	—	—	A,D	C
12.	B,D	—	A	—
13.	D	C	—	A
14.	—	B	A	C
15.	A	C	D	—

Interesting enough, just listening is sometimes all that is needed to help others feel less distressed. And, in most instances, it is far better to merely listen than to direct, warn, criticize or disagree, or diagnose what is being said or the situation. Clergy know this. They know that on the occasion of the death of a congregant, when everyone is really at a loss as to what to say, simply placing an arm around the mourner or a little hug can be more meaningful than any verbal communication. The following activity will help you practice listening and sharpen that skill.

ACTIVITY: REFLECTIVE LISTENING

In order to be able to communicate well, you need to acquire certain skills. This activity helps you learn how to employ reflective listening, acknowledge feelings expressed to you, and use "I" statements. *Reflective Listening:* To demonstrate that you are listening to someone, you can paraphrase what he or she has said and what you think that person is feeling. Paraphrasing uses other words than those said but have the same meaning. For example, if you paraphrased the statement, "What a rotten day!" you might say, "It seems that your day was really horrendous." In this way, the other person will know that you listened. Practice this reflective listening by rephrasing the following statements:

1.   I'm really feeling stressed out.

   _____

2.   My instructors are so unsympathetic that I don't know if I'll do well in school this semester.

   _____

56

3.   Cindy and I are not getting along very well lately.

_____

One way you might have reflected these statements back to the person communicating them is

1.   So much is happening that you obviously feel uptight and tense.
2.   It sounds like you're worried you won't get good grades this semester and that you can't expect any help from your teachers. That must be very frustrating and scary.
3.   You're worried about the future of your relationship with Cindy and what you can do to improve it, aren't you?

Acknowledging Feelings: When someone communicates feelings to you, it is best to acknowledge those feelings and accept them. For example, if I said, "I'm really upset that you would do such a thing," you might respond, "You seem disappointed and angry with me." In this way, you are recognizing that I have certain feelings and accepting that they exist. That doesn't mean that you think those feelings are warranted, only that you acknowledge their existence. Try responding to the following feeling statements with an acknowledgment of them:

1.   I get depressed every time I think of the death of my father.

_____

2.   I'll never be able to get up in front of the class and give that report with everyone looking at me.

_____

3.   I don't have very much confidence in myself.

_____

One way you might have made an acknowledging response to these statements is

1.   Your father's death has affected you greatly, even to this day. I imagine I'll react the same way when my father dies.
2.   Your feelings of anxiety and self-doubt are quite understandable. I experience these same feelings when I have to speak in front of a bunch of people.
3.   It must feel terrible not trusting your abilities. I feel for you.

"I" Statements: When you communicate by talking about the other person's behavior, that person is liable to feel defensive. One way to prevent that reaction is to use "I" statements. For example, if you want to complain about my not spending enough time with you, you could say, "You don't spend enough time with me and I'm really upset about that." Then, I have to defend not spending enough time with you. Instead, you could say, "I get upset when people I care for don't spend enough time with me." I'll know what you mean but will be more likely to consider that statement as a piece of information you're providing rather than a specific complaint requiring a justification of my behavior to you. Reword the following statements so they are "I" statements:

1. You require too much work in this class and I don't think that's fair.

   _____

2. I don't get the sense that you care about me because you are always looking away when I speak to you.

   _____

3. You aren't even sensitive enough to put your arm around me when I'm opening up to you.

   _____

One way you might have reworded these statements is

1. When so much work is required that it doesn't seem it can ever be done in the time allotted, I feel as though I'm being treated unfairly.
2. When someone I'm speaking to doesn't look directly at me, I get the feeling that person doesn't care about me.
3. When I open up to someone and that person doesn't express enough concern to make physical contact with me—such as putting an arm around me—I don't feel as though that person is very sensitive or even cares very much about me.

Section **VI**   **Perception Interventions: Responding to Feelings of Stress**

A friend of mine was presiding over a session at a conference involving several speakers. After the first presenter was through and a polite round of applause was offered, the second speaker approached the podium and soon, in mid-sentence, fainted. Later she told my friend how nervous she had been and the threatening thoughts that had invaded her mind. When my friend related this story to me, I could not help but recall a bar mitzvah ceremony I attended. The 13-year-old boy was in the middle of a prayer when his knees buckled and he dropped to the floor. In both of these instances, there was no physical threat. Rather, the threat was what other people would think of them. Would they "perform" well enough, or would they be thought of as incompetent? Fortunately for both the presenter and the bar mitzvah boy, they recovered and finished what they started out to do. This is not always the case.

Scale 6:1: How Often Do You Have Feelings That Are Generally Associated with Stress?

Each of us wrestles with feelings similar to those experienced by the two examples above. It may be related to making an oral report before a class or at work, asking someone out on a date, or attempting to join a group of which we would like to become a part. On these occasions, we flirt with rejection and the impact that might have on how we feel about ourselves, our self-esteems. If others do not think well of us, if they actually reject us, how can we believe we are worthy people? So, you see, your feelings have a great deal to do with the stress you experience and, as a result, your health and quality of life. The scale below measures the extent to which you experience feelings that are stressful.

> Listed below are descriptions of ways people sometimes feel. Think back over the past month. Place a check (✓) to show how often, during the past month, you have felt each way.

During the past month, how often did you feel . . .

	REGULARLY	OCCASIONALLY	RARELY
1. . . . that you could not deal with your life?	——	——	——
2. . . . lonely?	——	——	——
3. . . . annoyed by very loud noises?	——	——	——

	REGULARLY	OCCASIONALLY	RARELY
4. . . . that you had more things to do than you could handle?	_____	_____	_____
5. . . . that nobody really understood you?	_____	_____	_____
6. . . . nervous in a crowded place?	_____	_____	_____
7. . . . that you had no time to relax?	_____	_____	_____
8. . . . that you had no control of your life?	_____	_____	_____
9. . . . that too many things in your life were changing at one time?	_____	_____	_____
10. . . . worthless?	_____	_____	_____
11. . . . that people expected too much from you?	_____	_____	_____
12. . . . sad and disappointed with life?	_____	_____	_____
13. . . . that you could not do what you wanted to do?	_____	_____	_____
14. . . . that the things you had to do were too hard?	_____	_____	_____
15. . . . that all your work had to be finished at the same time?	_____	_____	_____

SCORING*

Assign the following point values for each response:

Regularly   = 3
Occasionally = 2
Rarely   = 1

Next, add the points and divide by 15.

---

*Source: Centers for Disease Control. *An Evaluation Handbook for Health Education Programs in Stress Management.* Washington, DC: Department of Health and Human Services, 1983, pp. 69–72.

INTERPRETATION OF SCORES

This is a scale that measures the degree to which you have stressful feelings. The maximum score obtainable of 3 indicates you frequently have feelings associated with stress, a score of 2 indicates you have feelings associated with stress only occasionally, and a score of 1 indicates you rarely have feelings typically associated with stress. Any score above 2 means you experience stressful feelings frequently enough to begin a conscientious program of stress management.

By this point, you know that these stressful feelings have the *potential* to make you ill, but they needn't do so. You can employ relaxation techniques or the other stress management strategies described in this workbook and prevent these potential negative outcomes. For example, rather than view oral presentations as threats, you can employ *selective awareness,* described in Section I, and consider presentations an opportunity to have people listen to your opinions. Rather than feel overwhelmed with your work, you could use the time management technique of delegating tasks to others, thereby reducing the burden. Or, rather than feel worthless, you could brainstorm a list of your positive traits and strengths on which to focus. You need not feel that you are a victim of stress or helpless in the face of it. You can do something about these stressful feelings and about managing the stress in your life.

The activity that follows will help you understand the stress you typically experience, how you usually react to it, and how you might react more effectively. In addition, it will help you identify stress early enough so your method of coping can have a greater chance of succeeding.

ACTIVITY: THE STRESS DIARY

Avoiding life's stressors should not be your goal. Instead, you should be striving for an optimal level of stress such that life is interesting while not being overbearing. Stressors should add spice to life, not illness or other negative consequences. Stress should be growth producing and encourage you to do your best, not create a threat that causes you to be dissatisfied with your life. To achieve these ends, you need to analyze the stressors you currently experience—both unusual ones and those that are routine—and then adjust your life so as to experience only an optimal level of stress. Keeping a stress diary will help. You can use the form on the following page.

Before you start, you need to have a clear understanding of the categories of the diary. For example, *routine stressors* refer to things that have the potential to cause a stress reaction and that occur often enough that they are predictable. Driving to work in traffic or arguing with your classmate or co-worker are examples. *Unique stressors* occur infrequently or are unpredictable. An argument with someone with whom you usually get along or an accident that ties up traffic on a road that is usually free of traffic are examples of unique stressors. Next, let's differentiate between *physical reactions* and *emotional ones.* Physical reactions are changes within your body, such as increased muscle tension and heart rate. Emotional reactions are feelings such as nervousness or anger. To continue, *means of coping* refers to what you did at the time you experienced the stressor to try to manage it. You also will cite what you might have done that would have worked even better *(means of coping better).* Relaxation techniques that you will list include any formal ones that you do (such as meditation or imagery) as well as anything else you do in an attempt to relax (such as listen to music or go out for a walk). Lastly, *body sensations* refer to any feelings or changes that your body experiences any time that day, such as headache, constipation, or stomachache. *Mind sensations* are feelings and thoughts that run through your mind (such as having a panic attack or feeling insecure) and differ from the emotional reactions you listed earlier in the diary because mind sensations are not specific to a particular stressor. Rather, they are general and may occur throughout the day. Now you are ready to begin your diary.

STRESS DIARY DAILY RECORDS

Stressors	Reactions		Means of Coping	Means of Coping Better
	Physical	Emotional		
1. Routine a.				
b.				
2. Unique a.				
b.				

Relaxation Techniques Tried	Effectiveness of Technique
1.	
2.	
3.	

Sensations:
   Body   Mind

Keep your diary for two to three weeks. To analyze your diary, answer the following questions and consider their implications for changes in your life so as to experience a more manageable level of stress.

1. What stressors do you frequently experience?

   _____

   Do you need or want to continue experiencing these stressors?

   _____

   If you do not, which routine stressors can you eliminate?

   _____

   How?

   _____

2. How does your *body* typically react to stressors?

   _____

   How does your *mind* typically react to stressors?

   _____

   Can your body's or mind's reactions to stress teach you ways to identify stress early in its progression so as to make it less harmful? How?

   _____

3. Are there any coping techniques that you use more than others?

   _____

   Do these techniques work for you or against you?

   _____

4. Are there any coping techniques that you believe would be helpful but don't use often enough? How can you get yourself to use these infrequently used coping techniques more often?

   _____

5. Are any particular relaxation techniques more effective for you than others?

   _____

   Are you experiencing difficulty in employing a relaxation technique? No time? No place? No quiet?

   _____

   How can you better organize your life to obtain periods of relaxation?

   _____

6.   Are there any *mind/body* sensations that you usually experience either preceding or following stressful events?

_____

    Are there ways to prevent either emotional or bodily sensations developing from your stress?

_____

    Summarize what you will *do* as a result of recording and analyzing your stress diary. Be as specific as you can. For example, rather than state that you will relax more, describe the time of day, place, and method of relaxation.

I will: _____

_____

_____

_____

_____

_____

_____

_____

_____

_____

_____

_____

_____

_____

Scale 6.2: How Much Do You Feel You Are Bothered by Stress?

When there is an automobile accident and the police arrive on the scene, they are required to file an accident report. In addition to their observations, the police officers record statements made by the people involved in the accident. Here are a few of the statements that have actually appeared on police or insurance company accident reports:

Coming home, I drove into the wrong house and collided with a tree I didn't have.

I collided with a stationary truck coming the other way.

A pedestrian hit me and went under my car.

The guy was all over the road. I had to swerve a number of times before I hit him.

I pulled away from the side of the road, glanced at my mother-in-law, and headed for the embankment.

To avoid hitting the car in front of me, I hit the pedestrian.

In my attempt to hit a fly, I drove into the telephone pole.

The pedestrian had no idea which direction to run, so I ran over him.

I had been driving for forty years when I fell asleep at the wheel.

I was thrown from the car as it left the road. I was later found in a ditch by some stray cows.

I was on my way to the doctor with rear end trouble when my universal joint gave way causing me to have an accident.

And you thought you had problems!! Humor can go a long way toward relieving stressful situations, but the best strategy is to avoid them in the first place. One indication of how successful you are at avoiding stressors is the stressful thoughts and feelings you have. The scale on the following page identifies the stressful thoughts and feelings you typically experience.

> Below is a list of problems and complaints that people sometimes have. Read each one carefully. Indicate how much that problem has bothered or distressed you during the past week, including today. Indicate whether it bothered or distressed you not at all, a little bit, moderately, quite a bit, or extremely. Circle one answer for each problem.

How much were you bothered by . . .	NOT AT ALL	A LITTLE BIT	MODERATELY	QUITE A BIT	EXTREMELY
1. . . . nervousness or shakiness inside?	1	2	3	4	5
2. . . . the idea that someone else can control your thoughts?	1	2	3	4	5
3. . . . feeling others are to blame for most of your troubles?	1	2	3	4	5
4. . . . thoughts of ending your life?	1	2	3	4	5
5. . . . hearing voices that other people do not hear?	1	2	3	4	5
6. . . . suddenly scared for no reason?	1	2	3	4	5
7. . . . temper outbursts that you could not control?	1	2	3	4	5
8. . . . feeling blue?	1	2	3	4	5
9. . . . feeling that people are unfriendly, or dislike you?	1	2	3	4	5
10. . . . having to check and double check what you do?	1	2	3	4	5
11. . . . difficulty making decisions?	1	2	3	4	5
12. . . . feeling hopeless about the future?	1	2	3	4	5
13. . . . feeling tense or keyed up?	1	2	3	4	5
14. . . . feeling uneasy when people are watching or talking about you?	1	2	3	4	5
15. . . . having urges to beat, injure, or harm someone?	1	2	3	4	5

	NOT AT ALL	A LITTLE BIT	MODERATELY	QUITE A BIT	EXTREMELY
16. . . . having urges to break or smash things?	1	2	3	4	5
17. . . . feeling very self-conscious with others?	1	2	3	4	5
18. . . . spells of terror or panic?	1	2	3	4	5
19. . . . feelings of worthlessness?	1	2	3	4	5
20. . . . feeling most people will take advantage of you if you let them?	1	2	3	4	5

SCORING*

Add up all the answers you circled and divide that sum by 20.

INTERPRETATION OF SCORES

This is a scale that measures whether you are avoiding stress, as indicated by the absence of common problems and complaints. If you scored higher than 4, you experience enough problems and complaints to indicate a high level of distress. If you scored lower than 4, you experience a manageable level of stress.

Glance at the items on the *Psychological Health* scale once again. Notice that they concern *feelings* and *thoughts,* not *actions.* And yet, these thoughts and feelings may govern what you do and the decisions you make, even when they are irrational. For example, you may know that it is irrational to believe that you have to be all knowing, perfect, and infallible. No one can be like that. And yet, you may be afraid to ask someone on a date for fear of rejection that would demonstrate your imperfection, or to take on a difficult assignment or college course for fear of failing, or to raise your hand in class to ask a question for fear that others will laugh at you when you demonstrate how little you know about the topic being discussed. The psychologist Albert Ellis wrote extensively of the influences of these irrational beliefs.

If you scored higher than 4, you should test the validity of the beliefs to which you responded "Quite a Bit" or "Extremely." Do these beliefs make any sense? For example, item 3 states that you are bothered by "feeling others are to blame for most of your troubles." Are others really to blame?

*Source: U.S. Department of Health and Human Services and National Institute on Drug Abuse. Research Issue 28. *Assessing Marijuana Consequences: Selected Questionnaire Items.* DHHS Publication No. (ADM) 81-1150. Washington, DC: U.S. Government Printing Office, 1981.

Most likely it is what you do that gets you into trouble, but it is easier to blame others. If you blamed yourself, you would have to take responsibility for your behavior and change it. That takes work. Some people would rather "disown" their behavior or troubles and lay them off on others. Then it is the other people that need to change, not you! The activity below helps you practice the skill of rewording "disowning statements" and take responsibility for your life.

ACTIVITY: MAKING IRRATIONAL BELIEFS RATIONAL

Reword each of the statements below to reflect a more realistic yew. The first statements are based on items on the *Psychological Health* scale you just completed. The first statement is reworded for you to serve as an example.

1.   Some situations make me nervous and shaky inside.

      In some situations, I make myself nervous and shaky inside by catastrophizing—thinking of the worst thing that could happen.

2.   I am often bothered by suddenly feeling scared for no reason.

      _____

      _____

      _____

3.   I often have temper outbursts that I cannot control.

      _____

      _____

      _____

4.   I am often bothered by feeling blue.

      _____

      _____

      _____

5.   I often feel that people are unfriendly toward me and dislike me.

      _____

      _____

      _____

6. I am often bothered by having difficulty making decisions.

_____

_____

_____

7. I often feel hopeless about the future.

_____

_____

_____

8. I often feel that other people are watching or talking about me.

_____

_____

_____

9. I am often bothered by feeling self-conscious with others.

_____

_____

_____

10. I am bothered by feeling that most people will take advantage of me if I let them.

_____

_____

_____

11. I am bothered by feeling there is nothing I can do to manage my stress.

_____

_____

_____

12. I am bothered by feeling that how much I learn in this course is dependent on how good the instructor is.

_____

_____

_____

Room is provided below for you to write three additional irrational beliefs that influence your behavior and decisions. Reword these as you have the previous 12 statements.

13. Irrational Belief:

_____

_____

_____

Irrational Belief Reworded:

_____

_____

_____

14. Irrational Belief:

_____

_____

_____

Irrational Belief Reworded:

_____

_____

_____

15. Irrational Belief:

_____

_____

_____

Irrational Belief Reworded:

_____

_____

_____

It is surprising how much a relief it is for most people to realize that they are in greater control of their lives than they ever thought they could be. This realization frees them of the shackles they created in their minds, it motivates them to make something better of themselves and of their lives, and it humanizes them to appreciate that it is as okay to fail as it is to succeed. Perhaps you have the same feelings now that you have, at least verbally, taken more responsibility for your life. Now, let's see if you can act on these newfound feelings and beliefs!

_____

Scale 6.3: How Much Do You Know About Anxiety Disorder?

Fear and anxiety are a necessary part of life. However, more than 19 million Americans face more than the "normal" amount of anxiety. How much do you know about anxiety disorder? To find out, circle the letter representing the correct answer or select True or False to the questions below.

1. Which of the following are disorders of the brain?
    A. stroke, epilepsy, multiple sclerosis
    B. anxiety disorders, schizophrenia, depression, alcohol addiction
    C. autism, anorexia, learning disabilities, dyslexia, migraines
    D. Alzheimer's, Tourette syndrome, Parkinson's, brain tumor
    E. All of the above

2. _True or False?_ Post-traumatic stress disorder, once referred to as shell shock or battle fatigue, is a condition that only affects war veterans.

3. _True or False?_ Someone who feels compelled to spend a great deal of time doing things over and over again such as washing his or her hands, checking things, or counting things has an anxiety disorder.

4. What is the most common mental health problem in the United States?
    A. depression
    B. schizophrenia
    C. anxiety disorders

5. Which of the following diseases/disorders are real medical illnesses?
    A. anxiety disorders
    B. diabetes
    C. high blood pressure
    D. All of the above

6. Which of the following are symptoms of an anxiety disorder known as panic disorder?
    A. chest pains
    B. dizziness
    C. nausea or stomach problems
    D. fear of dying
    E. All of the above

7. *True or False?* Anxiety disorders often occur with other illnesses.

8. *True or False?* Most people successfully take control of the symptoms of anxiety disorders by sheer willpower and personal strength.

SCORING*

The correct answers to these questions are

1. E
2. False
3. True
4. C
5. D
6. E
7. True
8. False

INTERPRETATION OF SCORES

Question 1: Brain research demonstrates that disorders as different as stroke, anxiety disorders, alcohol addiction, anorexia, learning disabilities, and Alzheimer's all have their roots in the brain. Every American will be affected at some point in his or her life, either personally or by a family member's struggle, with a brain disorder.

Question 2: Individuals who have experienced a traumatic event or ordeal such as a tornado, a rape or mugging, or a car wreck can be at risk for developing post-traumatic stress disorder (PTSD). Many people with this anxiety disorder repeatedly live the trauma in the form of nightmares and disturbing recollections during the day. They also may experience sleep problems, depression, or feelings of being detached or numb or may be easily startled.

Question 3: A person plagued by the urgent need to engage in certain rituals, or tormented by unwelcome thoughts or images, may be suffering from an anxiety disorder called obsessive-compulsive disorder (OCD). Most healthy people can identify with having some of the symptoms of OCD, such as checking the stove several times before leaving the house. But the disorder is diagnosed only when such activities consume at least an hour a day, are very distressing, and

*Source: National Institute of Mental Health. 2000. http://nimh.nih.gov/anxiety/adfacts.cfm.

interfere with daily life. OCD affects men and women equally. It can appear in childhood, adolescence, or adulthood, but, on the average, it first shows up in the teens or early adulthood.

Question 4: Anxiety disorders are the most common health problem in America. More than 19 million Americans suffer from anxiety disorders, which include panic disorder, obsessive-compulsive disorder, post-traumatic stress disorder, phobias, and generalized anxiety disorders.

Question 5: Anxiety disorders, diabetes, and high blood pressure are all real medical illnesses. Brain scientists have shown that anxiety disorders are often related to the biological makeup and life experiences of the individual, and they frequently run in families. Unfortunately, misconceptions about mental illnesses like anxiety disorders still exist. Because many people believe mental illness is a sign of personal weakness, the condition is often trivialized and is left untreated. The good news is that effective treatments are available for anxiety disorders.

Question 6: Panic disorders are characterized by unexpected or repeated episodes of intense fear accompanied by physical symptoms that may include chest pain, heart palpitations, shortness of breath, dizziness, or abdominal distress. These sensations often mimic symptoms of a heart attack or life-threatening medical condition. Left untreated, people with panic disorder can develop so many phobias about places or situations where panic attacks have occurred that they become housebound.

Question 7: It is common for an anxiety disorder to accompany depression, eating disorders, substance abuse, or another anxiety disorder. Anxiety disorders also can coexist with illnesses such as heart disease, high blood pressure, irritable bowel syndrome, thyroid conditions, and migraine headaches. In such instances, the accompanying disorders also will need to be treated. So, it is important, before beginning any treatment, to have a thorough medical examination to determine the causes of symptoms.

Question 8: Many people misunderstand anxiety disorders and other mental illnesses and think individuals should be able to overcome the symptoms by sheer willpower. Wishing the symptoms away does not work—but there are treatments that can help. Treatment for anxiety disorders often involves medication, specific forms of psychotherapy, or a combination of the two.

ACTIVITY: ANXIETY SEARCHING

Go to your university library and perform a literature search on anxiety disorder. Alternatively, perform this search on the Internet from your personal computer. Identify the following:

1.   The various types of anxiety disorders.

_____

_____

_____

_____

2.   Signs and symptoms of anxiety disorder.

_____

_____

_____

_____

_____

3.   Treatments and medications prescribed for anxiety disorder.

_____

_____

_____

_____

_____

_____

Scale 6.4: Are You Experiencing Excessive Anxiety or Depression?

There was a time when I was so anxious about giving speeches that I wound up sick to my stomach on the side of a road as I traveled to conduct a workshop. Barbra Streisand, in spite of a singing voice that thrilled millions, was so besieged by anxiety that she stopped performing live for over a decade; as did the singer Carly Simon. The great professional basketball player Kareem Abdul Jabbar also experienced anxiety and vomited often before games. The homeless advocate Mitch Snyder received the adulation of the country and a movie was even made about his life. Yet, Snyder was so depressed that he took his own life. As did President Clinton's friend and White House attorney. Whether rich or poor, famous or anonymous, talented or not, anxiety and depression have the potential to affect us all. The following *Personal Feelings Inventory* helps you see how stress may be manifested in anxious and/or depressed feelings.

> Please answer these items as they pertain to you now, True or False.

TRUE	FALSE		
_____	_____	1.	I have less interest than usual in things.
_____	_____	2.	I have difficulty concentrating.
_____	_____	3.	I am often sad or depressed.
_____	_____	4.	I have been uneasy or anxious in the past month.
_____	_____	5.	I feel depressed most of the time.
_____	_____	6.	I have trouble giving attention to ordinary routine.
_____	_____	7.	I have tried to avoid one or more situations in the past month.
_____	_____	8.	I have felt life wasn't worth living.
_____	_____	9.	I tremble; my hands are shaky; I feel weak at the knees.
_____	_____	10.	I have difficulty coming to a conclusion or decision.
_____	_____	11.	I feel overwhelmed with life.
_____	_____	12.	My thoughts dwell on a few troubles.
_____	_____	13.	My hands are sweating and clammy.
_____	_____	14.	I have kept up very few interests.
_____	_____	15.	Little if anything interests me.
_____	_____	16.	I feel hot and cold, and blush or get pale readily.
_____	_____	17.	I spend less time at usual recreational activities.
_____	_____	18.	I have butterflies or a sinking feeling in my stomach.
_____	_____	19.	I feel miserable or unhappy.
_____	_____	20.	I can't concentrate when reading.
_____	_____	21.	I am bothered by feelings of inadequacy.
_____	_____	22.	My heart pounds or flutters when I am uneasy or panicky.
_____	_____	23.	I have too little energy.
_____	_____	24.	I can't concentrate on movies or TV programs.
_____	_____	25.	I have fear of a particular object or situation.
_____	_____	26.	I tend to depreciate or criticize myself.
_____	_____	27.	I have a dry or coated mouth.
_____	_____	28.	I don't seem to smile anymore.
_____	_____	29.	I enjoy almost nothing.
_____	_____	30.	I enjoy doing little if anything.
_____	_____	31.	My fears prevent me from participating in some activities.
_____	_____	32.	I have had difficulty with my memory lately.
_____	_____	33.	I keep losing my train of thought.
_____	_____	34.	I have dizziness, faintness, and/or giddiness.
_____	_____	35.	I think about my death.
_____	_____	36.	I have difficulty in getting my breath and have a choking, tightness in my chest.
_____	_____	37.	My thoughts get muddled.
_____	_____	38.	I have trouble remembering something I have just read or heard.
_____	_____	39.	I seem to be slowed down in thinking.
_____	_____	40.	I have attacks of fear or panic and feel I have to do something to end it.
_____	_____	41.	I spend time sitting around or in bed.
_____	_____	42.	Recently I've been thinking of ending it all.
_____	_____	43.	I am uneasy when I go out alone or stay home alone.
_____	_____	44.	My memory is impaired.
_____	_____	45.	I avoid going out alone or staying home alone.
_____	_____	46.	My movements are slowed down.

TRUE	FALSE		
____	____	47.	I can't make up my mind.
____	____	48.	I have thoughts about killing myself.
____	____	49.	I am uneasy when in an enclosed space.
____	____	50.	I feel slowed down.
____	____	51.	I am discouraged about the future.
____	____	52.	I am uneasy when in crowds.
____	____	53.	I have lost interest in work.
____	____	54.	I avoid being in crowds.
____	____	55.	I can't concentrate on what people are saying.
____	____	56.	I get attacks of sudden fear or panic.
____	____	57.	I feel worthless.
____	____	58.	I have little interest in movies or TV.
____	____	59.	I spend almost no time at recreation.
____	____	60.	I avoid being in an enclosed space.
____	____	61.	I feel ill at ease with people in general.
____	____	62.	My future is bleak.
____	____	63.	I continually feel afraid of things.
____	____	64.	I get angry with myself.
____	____	65.	I have a diminished appetite.
____	____	66.	I feel slowed down in my thinking.

SCORING*

This scale contains two subscales: anxiety and depression. To score the anxiety subscale, add up the True answers you recorded for the following items:

4, 9, 13, 16, 18, 22, 25, 27, 31, 34, 36, 40, 43, 45, 49, 52, 54, 56, 60, 61, and 63

To score the depression subscale, add up the True answers you recorded for the following items:

1, 2, 3, 5, 6, 7, 8, 10, 11, 12, 14, 15, 17, 19, 20, 21, 23, 24, 26, 28, 29, 30, 32, 33, 35, 37, 38, 39, 41, 42, 44, 46, 47, 48, 50, 51, 53, 55, 57, 58, 59, 62, 64, 65, and 66

INTERPRETATION OF SCORES

This scale measures the amount of anxiety and depression you feel. Generally, the higher the scores, the more feelings of anxiety and depression you experience. For the anxiety subscale, scores of 11 and higher indicate you experience high levels of anxiety. For the depression subscale, scores of 23

*Source: A. F. Fazio. *A Concurrent Validation Study of the NCHS' General Well Being Schedule.* Vital and Health Statistics: Series 2, Data Evaluation and Methods Research; No. 73, DHEW Publication No. (HRA) 78-1347. Washington, DC: U.S. Government Printing Office, 1977.

and higher indicate you experience high levels of depression. Again, the higher the score, the more of these feelings you experience.

Both anxiety and clinical depression have a physiological basis. They also have a psychosocial component. For example, although panic attacks may be a function of hormonal imbalance, anxiety also can occur only in social situations or when having to perform (such as when required to give a speech before your classmates). Likewise with depression. Although hormonal imbalances may be the cause of clinical depression, all of us feel "depressed" or sad on occasion. If either anxiety or depression is a problem for you, consult with your physician to rule out physiological causes. These can be serious conditions. Once physiological causes have been ruled out, you might consider meeting with a counselor at your campus health center. Do not treat these conditions lightly. People have been so affected by them that they have attempted to end their lives. Help is available for whatever the cause is of these conditions. There are medications to correct hormonal imbalances and numerous forms of psychotherapy to respond to psychosocial causes.

ACTIVITY: BODY/MIND INCONSISTENCY

Anxiety is manifested in your body by reactions that can be measured. One of these bodily changes is an increase in heart rate. To demonstrate this reaction to anxiety, you must first learn to take your pulse, which indicates how fast your heart is beating. Place your first two fingers (pointer and middle finger) of one hand on the underside of your other wrist, on the thumb side. Alternatively, you can feel your pulse by either placing the first two fingers on your lower neck just above the collarbone or in front of your ear near your sideburn.

Now that you know how to feel your pulse, you can determine how fast your heart beats when you are at rest. To do so, allow yourself to relax for a couple of minutes and then determine your pulse count for thirty seconds. Double that number and you have your heart beats per minute.

Now, let's determine what changes occur in your heart rate when you are anxious. To do so, spend three minutes thinking of a situation in which you experience anxiety. For some people, a visit to the doctor is anxiety provoking. For others, it may be having a cavity filled or a root canal done by a dentist. Perhaps speaking in front of your class or interviewing for a job results in anxious feelings for you. *Vividly* imagine yourself in this anxiety provoking situation. Feel the sensations, see the setting, hear the surrounding sounds, smell the associated odors, and so on. After three minutes of imagining yourself in this situation, take your pulse again for thirty seconds and double it to determine how fast your heart is beating per minute. Most people's heart rates increase when imagining being in an anxiety provoking situation, much less actually being in one. Did you respond similarly?

Next, practice some relaxation technique (such as meditation, autogenic training, progressive relaxation, or something else that you do and find relaxing) for five minutes. Relaxation is the subject of the next section of this workbook. Therefore, if you are not familiar with relaxation techniques, you may want to wait until you finish that section before doing this part of the activity. After five minutes have passed, once again take your pulse. If you are like most people, your pulse count was lower than either your resting pulse or your pulse when thinking of an anxious image. In fact, some experts argue that you cannot be both anxious and relaxed at the same time. It is for this reason that relaxation techniques are helpful in managing anxiety. The next time you feel anxious, try focusing on your breathing, or imagine warm feelings in your arms and legs, or think of a relaxing setting such as a beach or a lake on a sunny day, or engage in some other means of relaxing. You will be surprised at how less anxious you feel as a result.

List situations in which you typically feel anxious below. Then plan to use some relaxation technique the next time you encounter these situations. With a little planning you will be able to anticipate and, therefore, better manage your anxiety.

I usually feel anxious when . . .

1. _____

2. _____

3. _____

4. _____

5. _____

_____

Scale 6.5: Do You Experience Panic Disorder?

Do you have a sudden burst of fear for no reason? Put a check alongside any of the problems you have during these sudden bursts of fear.

_____ I have chest pains or a racing heart.

_____ I have a hard time breathing or a choking feeling.

_____ I feel dizzy, or I sweat a lot.

_____ I have stomach problems or feel like I need to throw up.

_____ I shake, tremble, or tingle.

_____ I feel out of control.

_____ I feel unreal.

_____ I am afraid I am dying or going crazy.

SCORING*

If you placed a check mark alongside any of these problems, you may be experiencing panic disorder. The more check marks you placed, the more likely it is that panic disorder is a problem for you.

_____

Source: National Institute of Mental Health. 2000. http://www.nimh.nih.gov/anxiety/panri4.cfm.

INTERPRETATION OF SCORES

Panic disorder is a real illness. It can be treated with medicine and therapy. People with panic disorder feel suddenly terrified for no apparent reason. These frequent outbursts of panic are called panic attacks. During a panic attack, people have scary physical feelings like a fast heartbeat, trouble breathing, or dizziness. Panic attacks can happen at any time and any place without warning. They often happen in grocery stores, malls, or crowds or while traveling. People who experience panic attacks live in constant fear of another attack and may stay away from places where they experienced panic attacks previously. For some people, fear takes over their lives and they are unable to leave their homes. Panic attacks do not last long, but they are so scary they feel like they go on forever.

ACTIVITY: DESENSITIZING SYSTEMATICALLY

There are several effective ways of treating panic disorder, some of which a person can engage in by him- or herself. For example, you can adjust your life to avoid the stimulus that provokes the panic attack. Avoiding crowds is one adjustment that could prevent these attacks. However, avoiding crowds may mean not shopping at the mall, not attending movies and shows in theaters, not going to a concert at which many people will be in attendance, or not taking a lecture course even though the subject matter may interest you. This adjustment—avoiding crowds—is therefore dysfunctional. It results in the quality and happiness and enjoyment of life being diminished. A better approach is to confront the stimulus that provokes the panic attack a little at a time. Systematic desensitization is a technique that does that.

The first step is to identify situations in which you panic. Next, develop a fear hierarchy—a list of events that take you from a safe place to actually engaged in the situation or activity that makes you anxious. For example, if crowds provoke panic, the first step on your fear hierarchy might be receiving an invitation to attend a concert, and the last step would be sitting at the concert in the midst of a crowd of people. Develop your fear hierarchy below:

1. _____

2. _____

3. _____

4. _____

5. _____

6. _____

7. _____

8. _____

9. _____

10. _____

Now that you have your fear hierarchy, imagine doing the first step. If you can do that without feeling panic or physiological arousal, reward yourself by focusing on a relaxing image or revisiting in your mind a day that you really enjoyed. Then, move on to the next step on the fear hierarchy. In this way, you will be approaching the panic-provoking event a little at a time, in small steps, so eventually the situation does not produce anxiety or panic.

Scale 6.6: Do You Experience Obsessive-Compulsive Disorder?

Do you feel trapped in a pattern of unwanted and upsetting thoughts? Do you feel you have to do certain things over and over again for no good reason? Put a check alongside any of the problems you have experienced.

_____ I have upsetting thoughts or images that enter my mind again and again.

_____ I feel I can't stop these thoughts or images, even though I want to.

_____ I have a hard time stopping myself from doing things again and again, like counting, checking on things, washing my hands, rearranging objects, doing things until it feels right, and collecting useless objects.

_____ I worry a lot about terrible things that could happen if I'm not careful. I have unwanted urges to hurt someone but know I never would.

SCORING*

If you placed a check mark alongside any of these problems, you may have an obsessive-compulsive disorder. The more check marks you placed, the more likely it is that an obsessive-compulsive disorder is a problem for you.

INTERPRETATION OF SCORES

Obsessive-compulsive disorder (OCD) is a real illness. It can be treated with medicine and therapy. People with OCD have repeated, upsetting thoughts. They do the same thing over and over again to make the thoughts go away. They feel as though they cannot control these thoughts or behaviors. The upsetting thoughts and images are called "obsessions." Examples include a fear of germs, a fear of being hurt, and disturbing religious or sexual thoughts. The actions taken over and over again to make the thoughts go away are called "compulsions." Examples of compulsions include counting, cleaning, and checking on things. Many people with OCD know their actions are not normal, and they may try to hide their problem from family and friends. Some people with OCD may have trouble keeping their jobs and friends because of their actions.

---

*Source: National Institute of Mental Health. 2000. http://www.nimh.nih.gov/anxiety/ocdri2..cfm.

ACTIVITY: THERAPY RECOMMENDATIONS

Obsessive-compulsive disorder can be successfully treated, but it is a condition that requires the guidance of a mental health professional. Psychologists can provide therapy that can help someone with obsessive-compulsive disorder, and psychiatrists can provide therapy and medications that can help. If you think you have obsessive-compulsive disorder, consult with your family physician for a recommendation of a therapist, or friends or family members who have experienced therapy and can recommend a therapist they thought was effective in helping them with their situation. Alternatively, you can ask your instructor or a mental health specialist at your campus health center for a recommendation.

Scale 6.7: Are You Experiencing Post-Traumatic Stress Disorder?

Have you lived through a very scary and dangerous event? Put a check alongside any of the problems you have experienced.

_____ I feel like the terrible event is happening all over again.

_____ I have nightmares and scary memories of the terrifying event.

_____ I stay away from places that remind me of the event.

_____ I jump and feel very upset when something happens without warning.

_____ I have a hard time trusting or feeling close to people.

_____ I get mad easily.

_____ I feel guilty because others died and I lived.

_____ I have trouble sleeping and my muscles are tense.

SCORING*

If you placed a check mark alongside any of these problems, you may be experiencing post-traumatic stress disorder. The more check marks you placed, the more likely it is that post-traumatic stress disorder is a problem for you.

INTERPRETATION OF SCORES

Post-traumatic stress disorder (PTSD) is a real illness. People may develop PTSD after living through a terrible and scary experience. PTSD can be treated with medicine or therapy. People can experience

---

*Source: National Institute of Mental Health. 2000. http://www.nimh.nih.gov/anxiety/ptsd.pdf.

PTSD after having been raped or sexually abused; hit or harmed by someone in their family; a victim of a violent crime; in an airplane or car crash; in a hurricane, tornado, or fire; in a war, or in an event in which they thought they would be killed or after having seen any of these events. Those experiencing PTSD often have nightmares or scary thoughts about the terrible experience. They also may stay away from anything that reminds them of their frightening experience. People suffering from PTSD also may feel angry and unable to care about or trust other people, and may feel upset when something happens without warning.

ACTIVITY: DEBRIEFING TRAUMA

As with obsessive-compulsive disorder, post-traumatic stress disorder can be successfully treated, but it, too, requires the guidance of a mental health professional. Psychologists and psychiatrists can provide therapy that helps to place the threat of a reoccurrence of the situation more realistically. Part of the therapy might involve safely, and in small steps, encountering the situation. Systemic desensitization, described during the discussion of panic disorder, can be one vehicle to accomplish this task. Medications also can be prescribed to help treat post-traumatic stress disorder. If you think you have post-traumatic stress disorder, consult with your family physician for a recommendation of a therapist, or friends or family members who may know an effective therapist. You also may be able to obtain a recommendation of a therapist from your instructor or a mental health specialist at your campus health center.

To begin to understand your post-traumatic stress disorder, answer the following questions:

1. What was the worst part of the experience?

   _____

   _____

   _____

2. How likely is it that this event will reoccur?

   _____

   _____

   _____

3. How can you decrease the likelihood that this event will reoccur?

   _____

   _____

   _____

4.   What effect does your fear of a reoccurrence of the event have on the quality of your life?

_____

_____

_____

5.   Who can you speak with to share your fears and concerns?

_____

_____

_____

_____

Scale 6.8: Do You Have Social Phobia?

Do you feel afraid and uncomfortable when you are around other people? Is it hard for you to be at work or school? Put a check alongside any of the problems you have experienced.

_____   I have an intense fear that I will do or say something and embarrass myself in front of other people.

_____   I am always afraid of making a mistake and being watched and judged by other people.

_____   My fear of embarrassment makes me avoid doing things I want to do or speaking to people.

_____   I worry for days or weeks before I meet new people.

_____   I blush, sweat a lot, tremble, or feel like I have to throw up before and during an event where I am with new people.

_____   I usually stay away from social situations such as school events and making speeches.

_____   I often drink to try to make these fears go away.

SCORING*

If you placed a check mark alongside any of these problems, you may have social phobia. The more check marks you placed, the more likely it is that social phobia is a problem for you.

_____

*Source: National Institute of Mental Health. 2000. http://www.nimh.nih.gov/anxiety/sophri4.cfm.

INTERPRETATION OF SCORES

Social phobia is a real illness. Over 5.3 million Americans have social phobia. It can be treated with medicine and therapy. People with social phobia are very worried about embarrassing themselves in front of other people. Their fears may be so serious that they cannot do everyday things. They may have a very hard time talking to people at work or school on some days. They may worry they will blush and shake in front of other people, and may believe other people are waiting for them to make a mistake. Even talking on the telephone, signing a check at the store, or using a public restroom can make them afraid. Many people are a little nervous before they meet other people or give a speech. However, those with social phobia worry for weeks beforehand and may do anything to avoid these situations.

ACTIVITY: DECONSTRUCTING SOCIAL FEARS

The first step in responding to social phobia is recognizing in which situations it occurs and the reasoning you use to make yourself anxious. Answer the following questions to get a better understanding of your fear in social situations:

Place a check alongside any of the following social situations in which you experience anxiety.

_____ Meeting new people

_____ Having to speak before other people, such as a speech

_____ Asking someone out

_____ Speaking on the telephone

_____ Being at a party

_____ Speaking with a professor

Below, list other social situations in which you become anxious.

_____

_____

_____

_____

_____

Place a check alongside any of the following reasons you become anxious in these situations.

_____ I am afraid I will make a mistake.

_____ I am concerned that I will embarrass myself.

_____ I fear people will see me for who I really am and will not respect me.

_____ I fear people will reject me.

_____ I am concerned that I will demonstrate my ineptitude.

_____ I am concerned that people will think I am a fool.

Below, list other reasons you become anxious in social situations.

_____

_____

_____

_____

_____

Section VII Emotional Arousal Interventions: Relaxation Training

I was recently asked by an advertising and marketing professional association to conduct a stress management workshop for its members. Having conducted numerous stress management workshops, I can usually guess what the group is interested in and the needs they will express. However, this workshop was different. Someone once said to expect the unexpected, and from now on I will.

The workshop was proceeding as planned. I discussed the nature of stress, its effects, and how to manage it. Nearing the end of the time I had with the group of approximately 100 advertisers and marketers, I asked if there were any questions. From the rear of the room a woman raised her hand, waving it to make sure she was noticed. "What do you do about the death of your child?" she asked. Now, had this been asked privately after the workshop, I would not have been surprised. These are the kinds of questions people often come up to ask me after a presentation. But, when it was asked in front of 100 of her professional colleagues, I was taken aback. I responded by telling her that there was nothing of which I was aware that could ever alleviate that kind of stress—that time would make it less painful but offer no solution. I continued that there were things to do, though, that could offer periods of relief, and I proceeded to discuss relaxation techniques. At the conclusion of the workshop, I made sure to seek out this woman and discuss her situation with her in greater detail. Fortunately, she attended the workshop with some men and women with whom she worked and I was able to gather them for a cup of coffee and some discussion, with my agenda being to provide an ongoing outlet for this woman to share her feelings.

Although your need to engage in relaxation may not be as vital and immediate as it was for this woman, it still exists. Can you satisfy that need? Do you know about, and can you employ, relaxation techniques? This section will help you do that.

Scale 7.1: How Much Do You Know About Relaxation Techniques?

Each of us does something to relax. At the end of a particularly stressful day, we might watch television, exercise, seek solace from a friend or relative, or listen to music. These methods of relaxing work for a lot of people, although their effects are difficult to document. In addition, there are other relaxation techniques that have been well researched and whose effects are well documented. Among these are imagery, meditation, autogenics, and progressive relaxation. Others include yoga, body scanning, and the quieting reflex.

What do you do to relax? Does it work? Do you know about other methods of relaxing so you can make an informed choice about which method to use? The *Relaxation Techniques Knowledge Test* measures how much you know about these other ways of relaxing.

> There are many different ways that people can relax. This scale measures the degree to which you are familiar with those relaxation techniques. Read each item. Circle the letter of the most accurate and best answer provided.

1. When people engage in autogenic training, they:
   A. repeat a word over and over in their mind.
   B. imagine their arms and legs are heavy and warm.
   C. tense and relax muscles throughout their bodies.
   D. think of a relaxing setting.

2. When using yoga as a way to relax, you should:
   A. find a part of your body that is relaxed and transfer that feeling to a less relaxed part.
   B. focus on your breathing and body position.
   C. use a machine to tell you how tense you are.
   D. breathe by expanding your abdomen.

3. When using repetitive prayer as a way to relax, you:
   A. smile inside.
   B. send a wave of relaxation to the parts of your body that feel tense.
   C. repeat words in cadence.
   D. breathe by expanding your chest.

4. When people employ progressive relaxation, they:
   A. repeat a word over and over in their mind.
   B. imagine their arms and legs are heavy and warm.
   C. tense and relax muscles throughout their bodies.
   D. think of a relaxing setting.

5. To employ biofeedback as an aid in relaxing, you should:
   A. find a part of your body that is relaxed and transfer that feeling to a less relaxed part.
   B. focus on your breathing and body position.
   C. use a machine to tell you how tense you are.
   D. breathe by expanding your abdomen.

6. As part of the instant calming sequence, you:
   A. smile inside.
   B. send a wave of relaxation to parts of your body that feel tense.
   C. repeat words in cadence.
   D. breathe by expanding your chest.

7. When people use some form of imagery to relax, they:
   A. repeat a word over and over in their mind.
   B. imagine their arms and legs are heavy and warm.
   C. tense and relax muscles throughout their bodies.
   D. think of a relaxing setting.

8. To use body scanning to relax, you should:
   A. find a part of your body that is relaxed and transfer that feeling to a less relaxed part.
   B. focus on your breathing and body position.
   C. use a machine to tell you how tense you are.
   D. breathe by expanding your abdomen.

9.   When people meditate, they:
      A.   repeat a word over and over in their mind.
      B.   imagine their arms and legs are heavy and warm.
      C.   tense and relax muscles throughout their bodies.
      D.   think of a relaxing setting.

10.   When you employ thoracic breathing, you:
      A.   smile inside.
      B.   send a wave of relaxation to the parts of your body that feel tense.
      C.   repeat words in cadence.
      D.   breathe by expanding your chest.

11.   To use diaphragmatic breathing as a means of relaxing, you should:
      A.   find a part of your body that is relaxed and transfer that feeling to a less relaxed part.
      B.   focus on your breathing and body position.
      C.   use a machine to tell you how tense you are.
      D.   breathe by expanding your abdomen.

12.   One step of the quieting reflex is to:
      A.   smile inside.
      B.   send a wave of relaxation to the parts of your body that feel tense.
      C.   repeat words in cadence.
      D.   breathe by expanding your chest.

13.   When meditating, you can focus on something either repetitive or unchanging.
      A.   true
      B.   false

14.   Autogenic training was developed by:
      A.   Edmund Jacobson.
      B.   Johannes Schultz.
      C.   Robert Cooper.
      D.   Charles Stroebel.

15.   Progressive relaxation was developed by:
      A.   Edmund Jacobson.
      B.   Johannes Schultz.
      C.   Robert Cooper.
      D.   Charles Stroebel.

16.   The quieting reflex was developed by:
      A.   Edmund Jacobson.
      B.   Johannes Schultz.
      C.   Robert Cooper.
      D.   Charles Stroebel.

17. Instant calming sequence was developed by:
    A. Edmund Jacobson.
    B. Johannes Schultz.
    C. Robert Cooper.
    D. Charles Stroebel.

18. For biofeedback to be useful, the feedback must be:
    A. instantaneous.
    B. accurate.
    C. A and B above.
    D. Neither A nor B above.

19. For autogenic training to be successful in relaxing a person, that person must be:
    A. highly motivated.
    B. other-directed and other-controlled.
    C. A and B above.
    D. Neither A nor B above.

20. The goal of relaxation techniques is to bring about:
    A. a hypermetabolic state.
    B. enhanced muscle tonus.
    C. an increased heart rate.
    D. a hypometabolic state.

SCORING

Assign yourself one point for each of the following correct responses:

1.	B	6.	B	11.	D	16.	D
2.	B	7.	D	12.	A	17.	C
3.	C	8.	A	13.	A	18.	C
4.	C	9.	A	14.	B	19.	A
5.	C	10.	D	15.	A	20.	D

INTERPRETATION OF SCORES

The highest obtainable score is 20 and the lowest is zero. If you scored higher than 13, you probably have sufficient knowledge of relaxation techniques to decide which method can be most effective in relaxing you. If you scored lower than 13, you need to learn more about the various means of relaxing before deciding which relaxation technique is most likely to be effective for you.

The information on the following pages briefly describes several relaxation techniques. To learn more about a particular method of achieving relaxation, either consult with your instructor and/or read one of the books or listen to the tapes referred to in Section II.

Meditation

Meditation involves focusing on something unchanging (such as a spot on the wall) or something repetitive (such as repeating a word—a mantra). To use the meditation technique taught by cardiologist Herbert Benson to elicit what Benson calls the *relaxation response,* repeat the word "one" (or some word you find calming) in your mind every time you exhale. Continue doing this for 20 minutes. When you realize your mind has wandered, merely return to repeating the word.

Imagery

Imagery can be guided or unguided. When guided, someone else determines which image you should keep in mind when trying to relax. When unguided, you decide what image would be relaxing. If possible, it is best to choose your own image since you have a better idea of what you find relaxing than does someone else. Some images that people generally find relaxing are sunshine warming the body, a day at the beach, a rippling lake, a walk in the woods, the surf rolling on the shore, birds flying through the air, a carpeted room warmed by a fire, and a sailboat floating on the water.

Autogenic Training

Autogenic training requires you to imagine your arms and legs feel heavy, warm, and tingly. By doing this, blood flow increases to these body parts due to a dilation (widening) of blood vessels in the arms and legs. This is part of the relaxation response. After the body is relaxed this way, the mind is calmed by adding images of relaxing scenes. Imagery that is part of autogenic training is called autogenic meditation.

Progressive Relaxation

Progressive relaxation teaches the sensation of muscular contraction by focusing attention on the feeling of the muscles as they are tensed throughout the body. It then teaches the sensation of muscular relaxation by focusing attention on the feeling of the muscles as they are relaxed throughout the body. Once familiar with the sensations of muscular tension and relaxation, it is easier to recognize when stress has resulted in tension and to transform that tenseness to relaxation.

Body Scanning

Even when you are tense, there is some part of your body that feels relaxed. Body scanning involves searching for that part and, once identifying it, spreading that sensation to your more tense parts. The relaxed sensation can be imagined to be a warm ball that travels to various bodily locations, warming and relaxing them.

Diaphragmatic Breathing

Relaxed breathing occurs as a result of the diaphragm expanding, as opposed to stressful breathing that is a function of the chest expanding. Relaxed breathing is called *diaphragmatic breathing.* To try diaphragmatic breathing, lie on your back and place your hands on your abdomen. As you breath, you should feel your abdomen rise and your chest remain fairly stable.

Quieting Reflex

With practice, this technique is said to relax a person in just six seconds. The quieting reflex is done as follows:

1. Think about something that makes you afraid or anxious.
2. Smile inside. This breaks up the anxious facial muscle tension.

3. Tell yourself, "I can keep a calm body in an alert mind."
4. Inhale a quiet, easy breath.
5. Let your jaw go loose as you exhale, keeping your lower and upper teeth slightly apart.
6. Imagine heaviness and warmth moving throughout your body, from head to toe.

Instant Calming Sequence
Another relaxation technique said to take just seconds to elicit the relaxation response is the instant calming sequence. Its five steps include

Step 1:   *Uninterrupted breathing.* In the face of the stressor, keep breathing smoothly, deeply, and evenly.

Step 2:   *Positive face.* Flash a slight smile as soon as you recognize you are being stressed.

Step 3:   *Balanced posture.* Keep your chest high, your head up, neck long, chin in, and in other ways balanced. Imagine being lifted from a hook at the top of your head.

ACTIVITY: YOU, THE TEACHER

One of the best ways to learn something is to have to teach it to someone else. Being concerned that you will appear knowledgeable, having researched the topic thereby acquiring a good deal of information about it, and having planned the best way to present this information to another person all lead to knowing more about the topic yourself. Recognizing this benefit of teaching, this activity requires you to plan to teach a relaxation technique to a class of your peers.

Using the information appearing above—although you are encouraged to seek out even more information about each of the relaxation techniques briefly described—develop a lesson plan for teaching one relaxation technique to your classmates. To develop this lesson plan, complete the following form:

LESSON PLAN

HINTS

Objectives refer to what you want your students to be able to do at the end of the learning session(s) that they could not do at the beginning of the learning session(s).

Content refers to what the students need to know or what skills they need to acquire to be able to achieve the objectives.

Instructional strategies refer to what will occur in the learning session(s) that will convey the content to the students.

Evaluation refers to what you will do to determine whether the students have achieved the objectives.

The learning objectives for this lesson are

   1. _____

       _____

   2. _____

       _____

   3. _____

       _____

Some of the content students need to know and/or skills they need to acquire to achieve the learning objectives for this lesson are

   1. _____

       _____

   2. _____

       _____

   3. _____

       _____

   4. _____

       _____

The instructional strategies I will use to convey the content to the students are

   1. _____

       _____

   2. _____

       _____

       _____

3. _____

_____

4. _____

_____

I will evaluate whether students have achieved the learning objectives by

1. _____

_____

2. _____

_____

3. _____

_____

4. _____

_____

You might consider actually teaching this lesson. If time permits, perhaps your instructor will allow you to teach it to your classmates. Alternatively, you can ask your local school or community center if you can teach it to youngsters who express an interest in learning about relaxation techniques.

Scale 7.2: Which Relaxation Techniques Are Effective in Helping You Manage Stress?

People try to relax in a variety of ways. Some people find a walk relaxing. Others enjoy a warm bath or a massage. Still others relax by knitting, building cabinets, working on their cars, or playing with their pets. Seldom do these people evaluate the effectiveness of their attempts at relaxation. Perhaps there is a better—a more effective—technique they could use. This scale measures the degree to which you believe a particular relaxation technique is effective for you.

This scale evaluates specific relaxation techniques and their effectiveness for you.

> Identify some way that you usually try to relax. That may be reading, exercising, watching television, or any one of a number of other ways that people try to relax. Next, read each item and apply it to that particular means of relaxation. Decide the extent to which that statement applies to that relaxation technique. Then circle the appropriate letter to the right of the statement. Use the following scale:
>
> VT = Very True
> ST = Somewhat True
> NS = Not Sure
> SU = Somewhat Untrue
> VU = Very Untrue

1.	It feels good.	VT	ST	NS	SU	VU
2.	It is easy to fit into my schedule.	VT	ST	NS	SU	VU
3.	It makes me feel relaxed.	VT	ST	NS	SU	VU
4.	It helps me to handle my daily chores better than I usually do.	VT	ST	NS	SU	VU
5.	It is an easy technique to learn.	VT	ST	NS	SU	VU
6.	I am able to close out my surroundings while practicing this technique.	VT	ST	NS	SU	VU
7.	I do not feel tired after practicing this technique.	VT	ST	NS	SU	VU
8.	My fingers and toes feel warmer directly after trying this relaxation technique.	VT	ST	NS	SU	VU
9.	Any stress symptoms I have (headache, tense muscles, anxiety) before doing this relaxation technique disappear by the time I am done.	VT	ST	NS	SU	VU
10.	Each time I conclude this technique, my pulse rate is significantly lower than when I began.	VT	ST	NS	SU	VU

SCORING*

Assign the following point values for each response:

VT = 1   ST = 2   NS = 3   SU = 4   VU = 5

Add up the total points and divide by 10.

_____

*Source: Jerrold S. Greenberg. Comprehensive Stress Management. 9th ed. New York: McGraw-Hill, 2006.

INTERPRETATION OF SCORES

This scale measures how effective a particular relaxation technique is in relaxing you. The maximum score obtainable is 5, the minimum score obtainable is 1. A score of 2.5 or higher indicates you believe this relaxation technique is ineffective, whereas a score below 2.5 means you believe this is an effective relaxation technique for you.

Some people prefer a method of relaxing that relaxes the mind, with the body naturally following. Meditation is such a method. Others prefer to relax the body, with the mind naturally following. Progressive relaxation is this kind of a method. Still others prefer to engage in activities to relax both the mind and the body. Autogenics accomplishes this by first relaxing the body with feelings of heaviness, warmth, and a tingly sensation in the arms and legs. Then, it incorporates thoughts of a relaxing scene that calms the mind. The activity below will help you determine which of these approaches to relaxation you most prefer.

ACTIVITY: RELAXATION EVALUATION

Try four of the relaxation techniques described previously—imagery, meditation, autogenics, and progressive relaxation—and evaluate each using the adaptation of the *Relaxation Technique Rating* scale that appears below. If you find that one of the relaxation techniques works for you, incorporate it into your daily routine. Just as you need regular physical exercise, so you need regular relaxation exercise. If you find that more than one of these means of relaxing are effective for you, choose one to try for a period of time (perhaps two weeks) and evaluate it with the *Relaxation Technique Rating* scale. Then try the second technique for the same period of time and evaluate it as you did the other. This will allow you to determine the more effective of the two. This is the relaxation technique you should predominantly use, but for variety you can alternate the other technique on occasion.

THE ADAPTED RELAXATION TECHNIQUE RATING SCALE

Try to relax by using four different relaxation techniques—imagery (IM), meditation (MT), autogenics (AT) and progressive relaxation (PR)—as described in the previous part of this workbook. Then, evaluate each of these methods of achieving relaxation by using the scale below. Place the number of the appropriate response in the column under each relaxation technique.

1 = Very True
2 = Somewhat True
3 = Not Sure
4 = Somewhat Untrue
5 = Very Untrue

	IM	MT	AT	PR
1. It feels good.				
2. It is easy to fit into my schedule.				
3. It makes me feel relaxed.				
4. It helps me handle my daily chores better than I usually do.				
5. It is an easy technique to learn.				
6. I am able to close out my surroundings while practicing this technique.				
7. I do not feel tired after practicing this technique.				
8. My fingers and toes feel warmer directly after trying this relaxation technique.				
9. Any stress symptoms I have (headache, tense muscles, anxiety) before doing this relaxation technique disappear by the time I am done.				
10. Each time I conclude this technique, my pulse rate is significantly lower than when I began.				

Next, add up all the numbers in each column for a score for each of the four relaxation techniques. The lower the score, the more effective you rate that method of relaxation. Practice the relaxation technique you rated most effective for several weeks to evaluate it over time. If it holds up, you have found a means of relaxing that you can use the rest of your life. If its effects seem to wear off over time, try the next highest rated technique for the next several weeks. If its effects, too, wear off over time, you might consider alternating these two techniques to alleviate any boredom or "sameness" you experience. You also might investigate other relaxation techniques for their effectiveness (for example, yoga, body scanning, exercise).

Section **VIII**   Deciding to Manage Stress: Using Systematic Decision-Making Skills

A student in one of my classes told me about his mother's encounter with her physician. During a routine medical screening, she was diagnosed as being hypertensive. In fact, her physician told her that her blood pressure was so high that it threatened her very life. When she related to her son what had happened, he asked what treatment the physician recommended. She showed him the medication she was instructed to take daily. Her son then inquired as to what caused her high blood pressure; whether others in the family are susceptible to this condition and whether they also should be screened; when she should take her medication, that is, should it be taken with food or water, after a meal or before; when she should be reevaluated and how often should these evaluations occur, and so forth. He was shocked to learn that his mother knew none of these answers. When he showed his concern, she told him that the physician had a lot of people in the waiting room and was very busy, and that she did not want to take up any more of the doctor's time than was necessary. Aside from not getting what she paid for (advice to accompany the diagnosis), his mother did not have the information she needed to make good decisions about her health. With adequate information, she, and you, can make systematic decisions that will improve the quality of your life. And some of these decisions can help you manage stress better. Will you—can you—use systematic decision making to manage stress? That is what this section of the workbook seeks to help you with.

Scale 8.1: What Do You Know About Systematic Decision Making?

When you need to decide what to do about a stressful situation, it would help if you knew a process to employ that enabled you to make a good decision. The *Decision Making* scale appearing below helps you determine how much you know about making systematic decisions and how much more you need to learn.

> This test presents descriptions of people who are trying to make decisions that may affect their health or the health of others. Read each item. Circle the letter of the *next* step that the person should take in order to be making decisions using a *systematic approach.*

1.   Katherine is slightly overweight and wants to go on a diet. Although she has tried to diet before, she has never had much success with the diets she has chosen. Now Katherine realizes she must choose a diet that isn't too difficult so that she will stick with it.

She discusses her desire to find a suitable diet with one of her close friends. Together they identify several different diet plans that may be useful for Katherine. Katherine thinks about how she feels about going on a diet. She then discusses the different diets with her family doctor, who points out the positive and negative features of each. They also discuss what Katherine will have to do in order to stick to each diet plan.

What is the best thing for Katherine to do *next* in order to use the systematic decision-making approach?

A. Discuss the different diets with another friend.
B. Select one of the diets.
C. Have her doctor select one of the diets for her.
D. Realize that she must choose a suitable diet.

2. William started smoking many years ago, before the dangers of cigarette smoking were known. Now he recognizes that his cigarette smoking is bad for his health. Although William knows that it might be difficult, he wants to quit smoking. Some of his friends who used to smoke have already quit. William is sure that there are many different ways to stop smoking. He wants to choose the way that is right for him.

What is the best thing for William to do *next* in order to use the systematic decision-making approach?

A. Call a smoking clinic to find out about its program.
B. Decide how he will quit smoking.
C. Make a list of all the possible ways he can stop smoking.
D. Think of one way he can stop smoking.

3. Cindy has been invited to a party where other people will probably be smoking marijuana. Although Cindy has never smoked marijuana, she is curious about it. She realizes that she must decide what she will do if someone at the party offers her marijuana. Cindy thinks about what she might do. After Cindy goes to the library and reads some books on marijuana, she decides not to smoke at the party. While at the party, Cindy is offered marijuana several times but turns down the offers.

What is the best thing for Cindy to do *next* in order to use the systematic decision-making approach?

A. Talk to her friends about smoking marijuana.
B. Read more books about marijuana.
C. Avoid the people who offered her marijuana at the party.
D. Consider whether she's happy about her decision.

4. Martin enjoys being active and tries to exercise on the weekends. He would like to exercise every day after work. Some of his co-workers go to a gym near his office. His wife jogs every evening at the local park.

What is the best thing for Martin to do *next* in order to use the systematic decision-making approach?

A. Think of one type of exercise he enjoys.
B. Start to jog after work.
C. Realize he must choose a regular exercise program.
D. Talk to his co-workers about the gym.

5. Phil works in a very busy office. He has a great deal of work to do and sometimes he is unable to complete it on time. Phil knows that he is under stress at work and he wants to find a good way to reduce it. He discusses his problem with some of his friends. He then makes a list of all the ways that he knows of to reduce stress at work.

    What is the best thing for Phil to do *next* in order to use the systematic decision-making approach?
    A. Get information about his ideas from the company doctor.
    B. Select one of the ideas on his list.
    C. Ask his doctor to choose a good way for him to reduce the stress at work.
    D. Realize that he must find an appropriate way to reduce the stress at work.

6. Mary wants to take her son to be immunized at a local clinic. The clinic is very busy. Her child can have an appointment only on a day when Mary has an important business meeting.

    Mary already has made a doctor's appointment in two months for her child's routine checkup. She realizes that she must decide whether to take her child to the clinic or wait and have her child immunized at the doctor's office. Mary thinks about her possibilities. She calls the doctor and the clinic to find out if it is safe to wait.

    What is the best thing for Mary to do *next* in order to use the systematic decision-making approach?
    A. Think about the possible choices available to her.
    B. Decide what to do about immunizing her son.
    C. Be aware that she must make a decision about her son's immunization.
    D. Complain to the clinic's staff that they aren't flexible enough.

7. Phyllis works for the Westinger Company. For the last few months, Phyllis has been swimming during lunch hour. She enjoys the swim and is pleased with the improvement in her health and appearance.

    Her boss now wants Phyllis to attend board meetings that are held every Monday, Wednesday, and Friday at lunch time. She tells Phyllis that attending the meetings will be important for her growth in the company.

    What is the best thing for Phyllis to do *next* in order to use the systematic decision-making approach?
    A. Choose between swimming and attending the board meetings.
    B. Try to convince her boss that she doesn't need to attend board meetings.
    C. Talk to her boss about the decision she must make.
    D. Realize that she must decide between swimming and attending the meetings.

8. Debbie has diabetes. She keeps her diabetes under control by eating a special diet.

    Debbie's new boss is having a dessert party in a few days and Debbie is invited. All of the guests are supposed to bring their favorite dessert. Debbie shouldn't eat sweets and desserts, but she doesn't want to offend her boss by turning down the invitation. Debbie realizes that she must decide whether or not to go to the party. She thinks about the options that she has and discusses them with a friend who also has diabetes. She calls her doctor to ask her advice about eating sweets just one time. She also thinks about whether she would be able to resist eating anything at the party if she went.

What is the best thing for Debbie to do *next* in order to use the systematic decision-making approach?

A. Decide whether to go to the party.
B. Have her doctor decide whether she should go to the party.
C. Sign up for a special baking class for people with diabetes.
D. Make a list of her possible choices.

9. Gary visits the doctor once a year for a checkup. At one checkup the doctor discovers that Gary's blood pressure is slightly higher than it should be. He wants Gary to use deep relaxation because that may lower Gary's blood pressure. If it doesn't, Gary may have to take a special medicine.

Gary recognizes that he must decide whether or not to use deep relaxation. He wants to follow his doctor's advice, but Gary understands that using relaxation may not lower his blood pressure. Gary makes a list of possible choices and the consequences.

What is the best thing for Gary to do *next* in order to use the systematic decision-making approach?

A. Decide whether or not he will follow his doctor's advice.
B. Talk with a friend who has high blood pressure about the effects of relaxation.
C. Realize that he has a decision to make about using relaxation.
D. Discuss the possibilities with his doctor.

10. Diane is going to make some big changes in her life soon. She will be moving to a new city to start school and she is nervous about it.

Diane has heard that changes can cause stress but that there are ways to reduce it. She wants to choose a way to reduce some of the stress she's feeling.

What is the best thing for Diane to do *next* in order to use the systematic decision-making approach?

A. Start a regular exercise program.
B. Discuss with her family the possible ways she can reduce her stress.
C. Decide on a way to relieve the stress she feels.
D. Have the family doctor choose a way for her to reduce the stress.

11. Bob is quite heavy. He wants to lose weight and realizes that he must decide how he's going to do it. He discusses the situation with his wife. Together they realize that Bob will have to either go on a diet, start exercising regularly, or do both. Bob calls his doctor to get his advice. The doctor says that regular exercise may reduce Bob's appetite so that it will be easier to stay on a diet. The doctor suggests that Bob try to diet and exercise. Bob, however, doesn't enjoy exercising so he decides to go on a diet only.

Bob tries to diet for three weeks. He's unhappy because he's not losing much weight and is often hungry.

What is the best thing for Bob to do *next* in order to use the systematic decision-making approach?

A. Think about whether he is satisfied with his decision to lose weight by dieting.
B. Read books about weight loss.
C. Stay with his diet for at least another week.
D. Start a running program in order to follow his doctor's advice about exercising.

12. Joe drinks a great deal of alcohol. He always has many drinks after work. Lately he has been drinking when he gets up in the morning. He knows that he has a drinking problem.

     What is the best thing for Joe to do *next* in order to use the systematic decision-making approach?
     A.   Enroll in an alcoholism treatment program.
     B.   Watch other people to see if they drink as much as he does.
     C.   Recognize that he must decide what to do about his drinking.
     D.   Realize that he will have to decide what changes to make in his life.

13. Margaret wants to stop smoking. She knows that there are many ways to quit and that she should choose the best way for her. She discusses the matter with a friend. They come up with several plans: (a) Margaret could stop smoking completely on a certain day or (b) Margaret could slowly reduce the number of cigarettes she smokes each day until she gives them up completely. Margaret calls her doctor to ask her doctor's opinion. She also talks to other people who have already quit smoking.

     Margaret decides to stop smoking gradually. At the start of every week, she reduces the number of daily cigarettes she smokes by one. Unfortunately, Margaret isn't too happy with her program and she has trouble keeping track of the number of cigarettes she smokes.

     What is the best thing for Margaret to do *next* in order to use the systematic decision-making approach?
     A.   Have her doctor choose a way for Margaret to stop smoking.
     B.   Think again about her decision to stop smoking gradually.
     C.   Stick with her decision regardless of how she feels about it.
     D.   Read some books about how to stop smoking.

14. Stan wants to get into good physical condition, even though he smokes and has not exercised in years. He is aware that there are many ways to exercise and that some ways are better than others. He wants to find an exercise program that will be comfortable and effective for him.

     Stan talks to some friends to find out what they do to get and stay in shape.

     What is the best thing for Stan to do *next* in order to use the systematic decision-making approach?
     A.   Decide on an exercise program.
     B.   Quit smoking before he starts an exercise program.
     C.   Read some books about the different exercises he has heard about.
     D.   Jog regularly because he enjoys being outside.

15. Tom has been on a low-salt, low-fat diet for several months. He is pleased with the diet, even though following it can be difficult. He does have to prepare most of his meals himself from fresh foods.

     Tom has been asked to go on vacation with some friends. He wants to go, but he knows that he won't be able to prepare his own meals. If he goes, he may not be able to stay on his diet very well. Tom realizes that he has a decision to make about going with his friends.

What is the best thing for Tom to do *next* in order to use the systematic decision-making approach?
A. Decide not to go on vacation.
B. Have his doctor decide if Tom should go with his friends.
C. Think about whether his friends would mind if he didn't go.
D. Consider the options available to him.

SCORING*

Assign yourself one point for each of the following responses:

1.	B		9.	D
2.	C		10.	B
3.	D		11.	A
4.	C		12.	C
5.	A		13.	B
6.	B		14.	C
7.	D		15.	D
8.	A			

INTERPRETATION OF SCORES

This scale measures how much you know about systematic decision making. Using the key below, you can evaluate your incorrect answers as being either

1. *Skipped Step*—a response that describes one of the decision-making steps that occurs after the correct step.
2. *Repeated Step*—a response that describes one of the decision-making steps that has already occurred.
3. *Ineffective Implementation of Correct Step*—a response that describes the correct decision-making step, but violates one or more of the step's effectiveness criteria.
4. *Ineffective Implementation of Incorrect Step*—a response that describes an incorrect decision-making step and violates one or more of the step's effectiveness criteria.
5. *Deflective Action*—a response that is unrelated to effective decision making and may deflect the decision maker from taking necessary action.

---

*Source: Centers for Disease Control. *An Evaluation Handbook for Health Education Programs in Stress Management.* Washington, DC: Department of Health and Human Services, 1983, pp. 118–128.

INCORRECT ANSWER CHOICE ANALYSIS

	Skipped Step	Repeated Step	Ineffective Implementation of Correct Step	Ineffective Implementation of Incorrect Step	Deflective Action
1.	—	A,D	C	—	—
2.	B	—	D	A	—
3.	—	A,B	—	—	C
4.	B,D	—	—	A	—
5.	B	D	—	C	—
6.	—	A,C	—	—	D
7.	A,C	—	—	—	B
8.	—	D	—	—	C
9.	A	C	B	—	—
10.	A,C	—	B	D	—
11.	—	B	C,D	—	—
12.	A	—	D	—	B
13.	—	D	C	A	—
14.	A,D	—	—	—	B
15.	A,C	—	—	B	—

ACTIVITY: LEGISLATING DECISIONS

Imagine you are elected as a state senator and are required to vote on a number of controversial issues. Each time you decide how to vote, you use a systematic method of decision making. Below, briefly describe how you would decide each of the controversial matters presented. Be more concerned with the *process* you would follow in making your decision than with the decision itself. What steps would you follow and in what order?

1. Should your state make abortion available to pregnant women? If so, under what circumstances? You need to decide whose consent should be sought. Who should have to pay for the procedure? Should parents have to be notified if the woman is a minor? Should the father of the fetus be told? Should his approval be sought? What other considerations are necessary?

_____

_____

_____

_____

_____

2. Should your state make surrogate mothering legal? If so, under what circumstances? You need to decide whether a woman should be allowed to be paid to carry the fertilized egg of another woman. Should the company that connects the woman wanting a child with the surrogate mother be allowed to receive a fee? What should be done with babies that are born and not accepted by the woman who contracted with the surrogate mother (for example, babies born with a birth defect)? What should be done with the surrogate mother who refuses to give up the baby once it is born?

    _____

    _____

    _____

    _____

    _____

3. What should be done with frozen ova that are not used during in vitro fertilization (test tube babies)? When a woman has difficulty becoming pregnant, eggs can be withdrawn from her ovary and fertilized outside of her body (this procedure is called in vitro fertilization). Because the first few eggs transplanted in a woman's womb usually do not grow and develop into a fetus, more eggs are fertilized than are necessary. The fertilized eggs not immediately transplanted arc frozen for use at a later time, if necessary. In that way, the woman is not subjected to another invasive procedure every time her eggs are needed. If she does become pregnant, what should be done with the frozen fertilized eggs that have not been transplanted? Should they be discarded? Should they be used with other women seeking to become pregnant? Who should make these decisions?

    _____

    _____

    _____

    _____

    _____

Discuss your answers with your classmates and instructor and have them help you evaluate whether the way in which you arrived at your decision was systematic.

Scale 8.2: How Valuable Do You Believe Systematic Decision Making Is in Arriving at Appropriate Decisions?

Just knowing about systematic decision making is not enough. You need to believe it is valuable or else you will not bother to use it. This scale measures how valuable you believe systematic decision-making skills can be in arriving at appropriate decisions.

> This survey is about making decisions systematically. Please respond to all the statements in the survey. Read each statement. Decide the extent to which you agree with it. Circle the appropriate letter to the right of the statement. Use the following scale:
>
> SA = Strongly Agree
> A = Agree
> U = Uncertain
> D = Disagree
> SD = Strongly Disagree

1.	People who make decisions systematically reach better decisions than people who don't.	SA	A	U	D	SD
2.	Systematic decision making takes too much time.	SA	A	U	D	SD
3.	People who use systematic decision making have greater control over the events in their lives.	SA	A	U	D	SD
4.	People make equally good decisions no matter how they arrive at them.	SA	A	U	D	SD
5.	Systematic decision making is too complicated.	SA	A	U	D	SD
6.	It is worth the time to make decisions systemically.	SA	A	U	D	SD
7.	A systematic decision-making process doesn't consider how people feel.	SA	A	U	D	SD
8.	People who use systematic decision making won't make hasty decisions that they will regret later.	SA	A	U	D	SD
9.	Systematic decision making is too intellectual.	SA	A	U	D	SD
10.	Systematic decision making helps people make the best choice when deciding important things in their lives.	SA	A	U	D	SD
11.	Systematic decision making only works when making decisions with a group of people.	SA	A	U	D	SD
12.	Systematic decision making is the best way to make decisions.	SA	A	U	D	SD
13.	Systematic decision making is easy when people learn how to use it.	SA	A	U	D	SD
14.	Only logical people have the skills needed for systematic decision making.	SA	A	U	D	SD
15.	Systematic decision making is not flexible enough.	SA	A	U	D	SD

16.	The effort involved in making decisions systematically is well worth it.	SA	A	U	D	SD
17.	It is too hard to get the information needed to make decisions systematically.	SA	A	U	D	SD
18.	Systematic decision making helps people think about their values when they make decisions.	SA	A	U	D	SD
19.	People follow through with decisions they have made systematically.	SA	A	U	D	SD
20.	People make their best decisions when they follow their first impulses.	SA	A	U	D	SD

SCORING*

Assign the following point values for each response:

	SA	A	U	D	SD
1.	5	4	3	2	1
2.	1	2	3	4	5
3.	5	4	3	2	1
4.	1	2	3	4	5
5.	1	2	3	4	5
6.	5	4	3	2	1
7.	1	2	3	4	5
8.	5	4	3	2	1
9.	1	2	3	4	5
10.	5	4	3	2	1
11.	1	2	3	4	5
12.	5	4	3	2	1
13.	5	4	3	2	1
14.	1	2	3	4	5
15.	1	2	3	4	5
16.	5	4	3	2	1
17.	1	2	3	4	5
18.	5	4	3	2	1
19.	5	4	3	2	1
20.	1	2	3	4	5

Next, divide the sum of your points by 20.

*Source: Centers for Disease Control. *An Evaluation Handbook for Health Education Programs in Stress Management.* Washington, DC: Department of Health and Human Services, 1983, pp. 213–216.

INTERPRETATION OF SCORES

This scale measures your belief in the utility of using systematic decision making. The maximum score obtainable is 5. A score of 3.5 or higher indicates a belief that using systematic decision making is useful. If you believe it is useful, you will be more apt to use systematic decision making.

As you use systematic decision making, you will find your values emerging. Prioritizing activities or deciding which option provides the most of what you seek involves weighing the different choices. Your weightings may be very different than someone else's weightings because your values differ. I have found no better way of demonstrating this than the activity that follows.

ACTIVITY: ISLAND HOPPING FOR LOVE

The story below describes the actions of five people. Your task is to rank these people in order, from the one you respect the most to the one you respect the least. There are two islands close together in the ocean, but because of sharks in the water it is impossible to cross from one to the other without a boat. On West Island there is one woman (*X*), two men (*A* and *B*), and a boat. On East Island there are two men (*C* and *D*), but no boat. *X* is in love with *C* and wants to go to him, but she doesn't know how to handle the boat. She asks *A* to take her to East Island, but he does not want to hear about her problems or become involved in them. He wants to be left alone.

B offers to take *X* to East Island, but only after she spends the night with him first. She agrees. The next day, after *X* has gotten over to East Island, *C* discovers the circumstances under which she got there and wants nothing to do with her.

D, on the other hand, doesn't care what she's done or why. He'll take her under any circumstances.

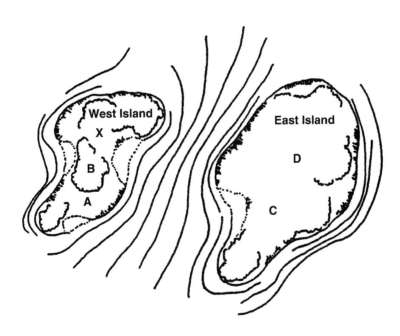

107

After you rank order *X, A, B, C,* and *D,* discuss your rankings with your classmates. Make sure to include the reasons for your rankings in this discussion. You will find that different people ranked these characters differently, and that is because different people have different values. Some of your classmates may value and admire *X* for her tremendous devotion, such that she would do anything to see the man she loved. Others may despise her for her infidelity. Some may value *A* for not "using" *X* when he had something she wanted. Others may feel *A* is selfish for not helping someone in need. Still others may admire *B* for going out of his way to help *X* even though he demanded a price, although there are classmates who may hate *B* for taking advantage of someone in need. And *C* may be admired for his emphasis on faithfulness by some and loathed by others for his lack of understanding of the predicament in which *X* found herself. Lastly, *D* may be ranked highly by those who value his willingness to help *X* when no one else would, or be ranked low because of being "so easy."

Knowing that values differ, do not be surprised when different people use systematic decision making and arrive at different decisions.

Scale 8.3: How Strong Is Your Intention to Use Systematic Decision-Making Skills?

Ann didn't know what a problem she was creating for her neighbors. All she was trying to do was be nice to Larry and Latisha's children by sharing with them a piece of cake left over from her birthday party. In spite of the cake being large enough to feed three hungry elephants and *their* offspring, the children argued over who would get what size piece. Larry was amazed. It seemed to him that the argument really boiled down to who would wind up with an upset stomach. Still, a solution was needed that would be fair to and accepted by both children. Here's what Larry decided: One child would cut the cake in two, and the other would select which piece to eat. If the child who cut the cake did so unfairly, the other child would be able to select the larger piece. The incentive, therefore, was to cut the cake into two equal-sized pieces so the second child could only select a piece of cake the same size as the one remaining.

Larry used systematic decision making to restore peace in his home. You can use systematic decision making to restore peace in your life. You will feel more at ease, experience more satisfaction from daily occurrences, and be better able to manage stress if you make good decisions. Do you agree? Do you agree to the extent that you actually intend to employ systematic decision-making skills? To find out, complete the *Would You Use Systematic Decision Making?* scale found on the following page.

This survey describes situations in which people might use systematic decision making. Read each statement. Circle Yes or No to indicate whether you would use systematic decision making in the situation described in the item.

If you circle Yes, then use the *Confidence* scale to show how certain you are that you would use systematic decision making in the situation.

The following examples show how the *Confidence* scale is used.

SITUATION	WOULD YOU USE SYSTEMATIC DECISION MAKING?	IF YES, HOW CERTAIN ARE YOU?
1. You are deciding on a career.	(Yes)/No	90
2. You are choosing where to eat lunch.	(Yes)/No	70
3. You are swerving to avoid a car accident.	Yes/(No)	____

Confidence Scale

10   20   30   40   50   60   70   80   90   100

| Very Uncertain | Somewhat Certain | Very Certain |

SITUATION	WOULD YOU USE SYSTEMATIC DECISION MAKING?	IF YES, HOW CERTAIN ARE YOU?
1. You are deciding whether to start an exercise program.	Yes/No	____
2. You are choosing a diet.	Yes/No	____
3. You are being rushed by others to make a quick decision.	Yes/No	____
4. You are choosing an exercise program.	Yes/No	____

SITUATION	WOULD YOU USE SYSTEMATIC DECISION MAKING?	IF YES, HOW CERTAIN ARE YOU?
5. You are being urged by others to make a decision in their favor.	Yes/No	_____
6. You are selecting a way to reduce your stress.	Yes/No	_____
7. You are deciding whether to see a doctor.	Yes/No	_____
8. You are making a decision and have many other things to do.	Yes/No	_____
9. You are deciding whether to take vitamins.	Yes/No	_____
10. You are deciding what to eat for dinner.	Yes/No	_____
11. You are deciding whether to use a nonprescription drug.	Yes/No	_____
12. You are deciding whether to start a diet.	Yes/No	_____
13. You are deciding what to do for a cold.	Yes/No	_____
14. You are making a decision while you have many things on your mind.	Yes/No	_____
15. You are deciding what to do to relax.	Yes/No	_____

SCORING*

Total all the confidence ratings made in conjunction with a Yes response and divide this sum by 15. Confidence ratings made in conjunction with a No response should be omitted from the analysis.

*Source: Centers for Disease Control. An Evaluation Handbook for Health Education Programs in Stress Management. Washington, DC: Department of Health and Human Services, 1983, pp. 220–223.

INTERPRETATION OF SCORES

The maximum score attainable of 100 represents your strong intention to use systematic decision making in a variety of situations, along with a high level of confidence in that ability. Scores lower than 50 mean you are unsure that you will use systematic decision making and that you can be effective in its use. Merely intending to use systematic decision making is not good enough here. You need to be confident that you can use it well or it is likely that you won't try.

ACTIVITY: A MODEL OF DECISION MAKING

Making decisions can and should be more systematic than is usually the case. If decisions were more systematic, better decisions would be made and the result would be less distress derived from poor decisions. This activity teaches one system for making decisions and encourages you to use this system for a decision you need to make.

The model of decision making we will use includes six steps:

1. *Perceive the problem.* Recognizing that the problem exists is the first step in solving it.
2. *Define the problem.* Narrow the scope of the problem so that it can be solved.
3. *Get ideas about the problem.* Generate as many possible solutions as can be thought up. Do not evaluate the solutions at this point. The idea is to accumulate as many as possible.
4. *Evaluate the ideas.* Evaluate each idea that has been generated in order to determine the relative merits of each alternative.
5. *Act.* Choose one alternative and put it into action.
6. *React.* Evaluate the action taken and determine whether it has been effective (if so, continue it) or ineffective (in which case, try to put another alternative into action).

To use this system, identify a decision you need to make and complete the form below:

DECISION-MAKING FORM

1. The decision I need to make is _____

    _____

2. More specifically, this problem entails _____

    _____

3. Possible solutions are _____

    a. _____

    b. _____

    c. _____

d. _____

e. _____

4.   The advantages of each possible solution are _____

   a. _____

   b. _____

   c. _____

   d. _____

   e. _____

5.   The disadvantages of each possible solution are _____

   a. _____

   b. _____

   c. _____

   d. _____

   e. _____

6.   The best possible solution is _____

   _____

7.   I will try this solution (when?) _____

8.   After trying the solution, I found that

   a. _____ It worked

   b. _____ It didn't work

9.   If the solution didn't work, I will next try _____

   _____

Section **IX** Specific Application: Intention to Use Stress Management Techniques

My father-in-law died recently and, as you can imagine, that was a very stressful time. My mother-in-law dwelled on the obvious tragedy of the situation. She would no longer have contact with the man with whom she shared close to fifty years of marriage. My wife took a different tack. She, too, recognized the loss of the man who fathered her for all the years of her life. Still, she could also focus on the way he died. He did not undergo any surgeries, he did not wind up with tubes sticking out of various cavities of his body, and he did not undergo many years of physical or mental incapacity. Instead, his heart merely gave out at the age of 77 and he died in his sleep. And that gave her comfort, making this stressful situation more manageable. I would like to take credit for the manner in which my wife was able to handle this stressful situation—you know, being married to a stress expert and all of that—but to be truthful, she has a way of finding the bright side in most situations.

Can you manage stress as well? This book is designed to help you do just that. Yet, it will not be very useful unless you actually intend to, and eventually do, use the stress management techniques presented here or in other sources to which you have been referred. Still, a prior question is your belief regarding how effective you believe you can be in managing the stress in your life. This section, therefore, concerns both your perception of your self-efficacy in managing stress and your intention to actually employ stress management techniques and strategies.

Scale 9.1: How Effective Do You Think You Can Be in Managing Stress?

"Okay," you may be saying to yourself, "Greenberg and his wife, and some of my friends and relatives can manage the stress they experience. But that is them, and this is me. I don't know if I can manage the stress *I* experience . . ." That is a fair statement and a valid concern. There are people who believe that some smokers can use a particular method to quit smoking and be successful but that they never could. Or that classmates can use a certain study method and do well in school but that they never could. This is the difference between *outcome efficacy* and *self-efficacy.* Your stress management outcome efficacy refers to your belief that there are stress management techniques that can help *people* manage stress better. Your stress management self-efficacy refers to your belief that there are stress management techniques that *you* can be successful using to manage your stress better. The *Keeping Your Cool* scale, found on the next page, measures your stress-related self-efficacy; that is, your perception of your ability to manage the stress you experience.

This survey describes various times when people might feel stress. Read each statement. Circle Yes or No to show if you would feel stress at that time.

If you circle Yes, then use the *Confidence* scale to show how certain you are that you *could manage the stress* from that situation. Stress management requires that you try to reduce excess pressures in order to increase your ability to lead a productive and satisfying life.

The following examples show how the *Confidence* scale is used.

SITUATION	MIGHT YOU FEEL STRESS?	IF YES, HOW CERTAIN ARE YOU THAT YOU COULD MANAGE THE STRESS?
1. You have just spent the worst day of your life.	(Yes)/No	20
2. You have just spent a typical day.	(Yes)/No	0
3. You have just spent the most relaxing day of your life.	Yes/(No)	_____

Confidence Scale

0   10   20   30   40   50   60   70   80   90   100

Very Uncertain	Somewhat Certain	Very Certain

SITUATION	MIGHT YOU FEEL STRESS?	IF YES, HOW CERTAIN ARE YOU THAT YOU COULD MANAGE THE STRESS?
1. You are trying to concentrate but you are constantly being interrupted.	Yes/No	_____
2. You have to do a very boring task.	Yes/No	_____
3. You have been thinking about someone who hurt you in the past.	Yes/No	_____

114

SITUATION	MIGHT YOU FEEL STRESS?	IF YES, HOW CERTAIN ARE YOU THAT YOU COULD MANAGE THE STRESS?
4. You have a neighbor who plays loud music all the time.	Yes/No	_____
5. You have several things to finish in a very short time.	Yes/No	_____
6. You are home by yourself and feel lonely.	Yes/No	_____
7. You are in a crowded bus and can't get to the exit in time for your stop.	Yes/No	_____
8. You keep thinking about an unpleasant experience.	Yes/No	_____
9. You have taken on more than you can do.	Yes/No	_____
10. You are waiting on the street for someone to pick you up, and you are getting cold.	Yes/No	_____
11. Although you have plenty of time, you are worried that you will be late for an important appointment.	Yes/No	_____
12. Your closest friend has left town and you feel alone.	Yes/No	_____
13. You are in a room that is extremely hot.	Yes/No	_____
14. You must buy a gift for someone and the stores are closing.	Yes/No	_____
15. You saw someone being robbed and keep imagining that it could happen to you.	Yes/No	_____
16. You have to wait for a delivery and you have nothing to do.	Yes/No	_____
17. Your friends keep asking you to do things you don't have time to do.	Yes/No	_____

SITUATION	MIGHT YOU FEEL STRESS?	IF YES, HOW CERTAIN ARE YOU THAT YOU COULD MANAGE THE STRESS?
18. You must get a prescription filled and you can't find a drug store that is open.	Yes/No	_____
19. You spend a good deal of time in a place that is very noisy.	Yes/No	_____
20. No matter how hard you have tried, you haven't been able to finish all your work.	Yes/No	_____

SCORING*

Compute the sum of the confidence ratings made in conjunction with a Yes response. Divide this sum by the number of Yes responses. The maximum score obtainable is 100. Omit from the scoring any confidence ratings for items to which you responded No.

INTERPRETATION OF SCORES

This scale measures how confident you are that you can manage stressful situations when they occur. High scores (over 50) indicate you are confident that you can manage the stress that you will experience. Low scores (below 50) indicate you do not believe you will be very successful managing the stressful events that you may encounter.

If you find that you are still unsure you can manage the stress in your life, share this feeling with your instructor. Your instructor can probably recommend some reading or exercises to hone your stress management skills. There may also be stress management workshops on campus or in the community in which you can participate. If you are so inclined, you can even write to me in care of the publisher of this book or at the University of Maryland for suggestions. I would be more than willing to consult with you. In addition, the activity below should be of some assistance.

---

*Source: Centers for Disease Control. *An Evaluation Handbook for Health Education Programs in Stress Management.* Washington, DC: Department of Health and Human Services, 1983, pp. 190–194.

ACTIVITY: BECOMING SELF-EFFICACIOUS

This activity will help you feel more confident that you can manage the stress you experience. Researchers tell us that there are several effective ways to increase self-efficacy. One of these is *modeling*. If you see someone else managing stress, you are more likely to believe you can manage it, too. All you need to do is model your behavior on this other person's. In addition, if you *practice* stress management skills—developing a history of using them—you will be more apt to believe you can employ them successfully. Lastly, if you employ social support—the assistance of other people—you will not feel left all alone to manage your stress. You will have others to consult with, to rely on, and to encourage you to be successful in managing the stress in your life.

Recognizing these strategies can be effective in enhancing your stress management self-efficacy, each is employed below.

I. *Modeling*

    A.   Identify someone you know who manages stress well

    _____

    B.   Observe this person over several weeks and list seven things he or she does to cope with the stress

       1. _____

       2. _____

       3. _____

       4. _____

       5. _____

       6. _____

       7. _____

II. *Practicing*

    A.   Choose three of the seven stress management techniques you observed the other person using that you are willing to try.

       1. _____

       2. _____

       3. _____

B.   Use one of these three stress management techniques this week, another next week, and the third the week after. At the end of each week, record whether the technique helped you manage stress. By the end of week three you should have found at least one technique you can be successful in using to manage your stress.

III. *Social Support*

A.   Identify two people who you feel comfortable asking to help you manage stress.

1.   _____

2.   _____

B.   List the three ways each of these people can help. For example, one person may be uniquely qualified by experience or personality to make suggestions regarding how to handle stressful events, whereas the other person may be able to exercise with you so you feel less distressed.

| _____ | _____ |
| (Person's Name) | (Person's Name) |

1. _____   1. _____

   _____   _____

2. _____   2. _____

   _____   _____

3. _____   3. _____

   _____   _____

C.   Next, ask these people to help you in the way in which you have identified they can be of assistance. Be prepared to negotiate with them to help in some other way if they feel uncomfortable or unwilling to assist you as you had envisioned. If one of these people is unwilling to help you manage stress, identify a substitute person, list three ways that person might help, and ask that person about his or her willingness to assist.

Now that you have modeled your behavior on someone whom you perceive as successful in managing stress, have practiced stress management skills, and have sought the social support you need, you can feel more confident that you can actually manage the stress you encounter.

Scale 9.2: How Intent Are You on Using Stress Management Techniques?

We conclude this book by giving you a chance to determine how intent you are on employing stress management techniques to help you cope with the stress of your life. This scale measures the degree to which you are committed to use stress management strategies.

This survey describes things that people might do to manage stress. Read each statement. Circle Yes or No to show if you intend to do what is described in the item.

If you circle Yes, then use the *Strength of Intention* scale to show how strong your intention is to do what is described.

The following examples show how the *Strength of Intention* scale is used.

STRESS MANAGEMENT STRATEGIES	DO YOU INTEND TO DO THIS?	IF YES, HOW STRONG IS YOUR INTENTION?
1. Eat something every day.	(Yes)/No	90
2. Go to a store this week.	(Yes)/No	70
3. Try to swim across an ocean.	Yes/(No)	_____

Strength of Intention Scale

10   20   30   40   50   60   70   80   90   100

Very Weak	Very Strong

STRESS MANAGEMENT STRATEGIES	DO YOU INTEND TO DO THIS?	IF YES, HOW STRONG IS YOUR INTENTION?
1. Find alternatives for goals you have been unable to reach.	Yes/No	_____
2. Stay away from crowded places if they make you nervous.	Yes/No	_____

STRESS MANAGEMENT STRATEGIES	DO YOU INTEND TO DO THIS?	IF YES, HOW STRONG IS YOUR INTENTION?
3. Do the most important things first when you have too many things to do.	Yes/No	_____
4. Find interesting things to do when you are bored.	Yes/No	_____
5. Use earplugs when you are in very noisy places.	Yes/No	_____
6. Avoid unnecessary changes when you have many other things to do.	Yes/No	_____
7. Look at the positive things in yourself and your life.	Yes/No	_____
8. Take one thing at a time.	Yes/No	_____
9. Get plenty of sleep every night.	Yes/No	_____
10. Talk about your problems with friends or family.	Yes/No	_____
11. Talk about your problems with the people who are involved in them.	Yes/No	_____
12. Balance work with relaxing activities.	Yes/No	_____
13. Use relaxation techniques.	Yes/No	_____
14. Get regular exercise.	Yes/No	_____
15. Avoid large amounts of caffeine.	Yes/No	_____
16. Try to identify what is causing your stress.	Yes/No	_____
17. Accept realistic goals for yourself and others.	Yes/No	_____
18. Avoid having many big changes come at the same time.	Yes/No	_____

STRESS MANAGEMENT STRATEGIES	DO YOU INTEND TO DO THIS?	IF YES, HOW STRONG IS YOUR INTENTION?
19. Get professional help if you feel too much stress.	Yes/No	_____
20. Accept what you cannot change.	Yes/No	_____

SCORING*

Total all the strength ratings made in conjunction with a Yes response and divide this sum by 20 (the total number of items in this scale). Strength ratings made in conjunction with a No response should be eliminated from the scoring analysis. The maximum score attainable is 100.

INTERPRETATION OF SCORES

This scale measures how intent you are on using stress management techniques. High scores (over 50) indicate you strongly intend to employ a number of stress management techniques to manage the stress in your life. Low scores (below 50) indicate you are generally not intent on using a variety of stress management techniques to manage stress.

Recognize that even if you do not feel as though you will use stress management techniques now, or this year, or next, there may be a future time when you decide you need to use them. Each of us experiences particularly stressful times in our lives. It may be the death of our loved ones, or getting fired from our jobs, or failing a course in college, or having a lover break up with us. For those of you who do not intend to use stress management techniques right away, this workbook has planted seeds that will sprout when you are ready. Keep this workbook available for that occasion.

---

*Source: Centers for Disease Control. *An Evaluation Handbook for Health Education Programs in Stress Management.* Washington, DC: Department of Health and Human Services, 1983, pp. 200–203.

ACTIVITY: THE WORRY GRID

For you to actually use stress management techniques, you need to believe they will be effective. The following activity is but one that has some real practical utility.

To begin, list as many of your worries as you can identify. *BIG* worries and *small* worries. Serious worries and insignificant ones. List every single worry you can; *as many* as you can. *DO THAT NOW* before proceeding with this activity.

_____

_____

_____

_____

_____

_____

_____

_____

_____

_____

Now let's make more sense of the worries you listed. Place your worries on the following *Worry Grid* according to the following instructions:

If the worry involves something you *Can Control* and that is Important to you, list it in Quadrant I.

If the worry involves something you *Cannot Control* but that is Important to you, list it in Quadrant II.

If the worry involves something you *Can Control* but that is Not Important to you, list it in Quadrant III.

If the worry involves something you *Cannot Control* and that is Not Important to you, list it in Quadrant IV.

DO NOT PROCEED UNTIL YOU HAVE LISTED EACH AND EVERY WORRY SOMEPLACE IN THE WORRY GRID.

WORRY GRID

	Can Control	Cannot Control
Important	I	II
Not Important	III	IV

Once you have listed all your worries on the Worry Grid, you need to check your work *carefully*.

Look at Quadrant I: Are there any worries listed here that are either really beyond your control or are really not very important? If so, delete that worry from Quadrant I and move it to the appropriate quadrant in the grid.

What you are now left with in Quadrant I are only those worries that are both important to you and over which you can exercise some control. Those are the *only* worries you need to focus on. Here's why.

Left in Quadrant II are worries that, while important to you, can be little influenced by anything you do since you cannot exercise any control over them. If there's nothing you can do, why worry? The worry serves no useful purpose and only makes you unhappy and distressed. It's like worrying about flying on an airplane. Once in the air, unless you know how to fly a plane, worrying does you no good. At that point, worrying only makes you nervous, increases your blood pressure and the serum cholesterol roaming about in your blood, and has the potential to make you ill. Why worry about things that you have no influence over? What will be, will be. Place an X through Quadrant II.

Left in Quadrant III are worries over which you can exercise some control but that are not very important to you. For these worries, the potential to get ill and elicit a stress response is not worth it. You yourself have said these things are not very important. If not very important, why worry about them? They're not worth the time or the energy and effort that worrying about them requires. What makes most sense in relation to these worries is to ignore them. They're just not important enough to waste your time, energy, and effort on them. Place an X through Quadrant III.

Left in Quadrant IV are worries both over which you cannot exercise any control and that are not very important to you. These worries are almost irrelevant. Who cares about them or, rather, who should care about them? Certainly not you! You don't consider them important and, even if you did, there's nothing you can do about them anyhow! Let's not even spend any more time on these. Place an X through Quadrant IV immediately.

Remaining are the Quadrant I worries. As we've said before, these worries are important to you and there *is* something you can do to influence events relative to these worries. Now that you've isolated Quadrant I worries from the others—others that aren't important anyhow, or if they are, can't be influenced—you can focus upon what *is* really important and about which you *can* do something. The other worries are no longer clouding the picture.

Next, you need to choose each of the Quadrant I worries separately and devise a plan to exert the control you stated you had. This will increase the likelihood they will turn out the way you desire. There are no guarantees that what you are worried about will turn out the way you'd like it to. However, you can increase the probability that it will work out as you choose. At least you know that doing something is better than doing nothing!

Spend a few moments to determine how best to exert the control you stated you had over Quadrant I worries.

Now go about putting your plan into operation.

You'll see how much better you'll feel and how much less worried you'll be.